BREAKFAST IN BED

Breakfast in Bed

more than 150 recipes for delicious morning meals

CAROL FRIEBERG

SASQUATCH BOOKS
SEATTLE

Note: All of the recipes featured in this book were originally published in Breakfast in Bed Cookbook (Sasquatch Books, 1990) or Breakfast in Bed California Cookbook (Sasquatch Books, 1997). Recipes originated from breakfast-and-beds and inns along the West Coast, from California to British Columbia. As eighteen years have passed since the first publication, we cannot guarantee that any of these great establishments remain open to this day.

Printed in Canada
Published by Sasquatch Books
Distributed by PGW/Perseus

15 14 13 12 11 10 09 08 07   9 8 7 6 5 4 3 2 1

Cover photograph: Kate Baldwin
Food stylist: Christy Nordstrom
Cover design: Rosebud Eustace
Interior design and composition: Rosebud Eustace

Library of Congress Cataloging-in-Publication Data

Frieberg, Carol
  Breakfast in bed : more than 150 recipes for delicious morning meals / Carol Frieberg.
    p. cm.
  ISBN-13: 978-1-57061-547-4
  ISBN-10: 1-57061-547-0
  1. Breakfast. 2. Bed and breakfast accommodations—Northwest, Pacific. 3. Cookery, American—Pacific Northwest style. 4. Cookery, American—California style. I. Title.

TX733.F753 2008
641.5'2—dc22

                              2007030252

Sasquatch Books
119 South Main Street, Suite 400
Seattle, WA 98104
(206) 467-4300
www.sasquatchbooks.com
custserv@sasquatchbooks.com

Cooking is like love. It should be entered into with abandon or not at all.

—Harriet van Horne

Contents

Introduction
ix

SCONES & MUFFINS
I

BREADS & COFFEE CAKES
27

PANCAKES, WAFFLES
& FRENCH TOAST
53

HOUSE SPECIALTIES
81

MORNING EGG DISHES
107

EGGS FOR A CROWD
133

SAUCES & SIDE DISHES
149

Index
175

Introduction

I have found that anything that imparts a little joy to my morning routine has a positive impact on the rest of my day. The simple act of sitting down to breakfast allows me to satisfy my hunger, savor the moment, and reflect some on the upcoming day. It is also an opportunity to connect and share time with a loved one, nourishing both heart and body.

For special occasions or simply to celebrate a lazy Saturday morning, what better gift than breakfast in bed? Whether it be a warm scone and herbal tea, or a beautiful breakfast tray delivering a cheese soufflé with poached pears and chilled champagne, it's the simple act of service that wins the heart. Admittedly, there have been mornings when nothing has made me happier than a steaming cup of freshly brewed coffee delivered to me in the bathtub. And a Sunday morning omelet made with someone else's loving hands still tastes better than anything I could have prepared myself.

Breakfast in Bed is a perfect resource to help broaden your breakfast horizons. From pancakes and waffles to quiches and frittatas, the recipes you'll find in this book are easy to prepare and easy to love. The recipes themselves have their origins from bed-and-breakfasts (from owners who know a thing or two about the meal, not to mention morning romance). As such, all the dishes here are deliciously tried and true. From Blueberry Sourdough Cobbler to Banana Buckwheat Pancakes, the recipes in this book will appeal to anyone who appreciates good food.

Whether surprising your sweetie with breakfast in bed, inviting your in-laws over for brunch, or taking a basket of scones to a neighbor, you now have an amazing array of wonderful breakfast ideas to share and enjoy. Have fun in the kitchen. Be good to yourself and those you love. And remember, you have it in your power to cook up a terrific day!

—Carol Frieberg

Scones & Muffins

CINNAMON GLAZED SCONES

CRANBERRY BUTTERMILK SCONES

DRIED CHERRY SCONES

DATE PECAN SCONES

OATMEAL SCONES

BERRY-FILLED SCONES

ORANGE CURRANT SCONES

FRENCH BREAKFAST PUFFS

FRESH BLUEBERRY MUFFINS

APRICOT CORNMEAL MUFFINS

RASPBERRY STREUSEL MUFFINS

OATMEAL PEACH MUFFINS

APPLESAUCE WALNUT MUFFINS

ORANGE APRICOT MUFFINS

LOW-FAT YOGURT MUFFINS

BANANA–OAT BRAN MUFFINS

GINGERBREAD MUFFINS

MINI LEMON MUFFINS

GINGER PEAR MUFFINS

APPLE CRANBERRY MUFFINS

PUMPKIN PIE MUFFINS

MANDARIN ORANGE MUFFINS

CRAN-BLACKBERRY MUFFINS

Cinnamon Glazed Scones

Twenty Scones

2 cups all-purpose flour

¼ cup sugar

1 tablespoon baking powder

½ teaspoon salt

½ cup golden raisins

¼ cup raisins

1¼ cups heavy (whipping) cream

3 tablespoons butter, melted

Cinnamon sugar (1½ tablespoons sugar mixed with
   1 tablespoon ground cinnamon)

Preheat oven to 400°F. In a large bowl, combine flour, sugar, baking powder, and salt; stir in raisins. Add cream until mixture clings together and forms soft dough. Turn dough onto a lightly floured surface and knead gently 10 times. Pat dough into a ½-inch-thick circle. Cut with biscuit cutter or heart-shaped cookie cutter. Place scones on a baking sheet lined with parchment paper (or freeze for future baking). Brush scones lightly with melted butter and sprinkle with cinnamon sugar. Bake for about 15 minutes, or until scones are golden brown.

Cinnamon Bear Bed & Breakfast
St. Helena, California

Cranberry Buttermilk Scones

Twenty-Four Scones

1½ cups (3 sticks) cold butter

4 cups all-purpose flour

½ cup sugar

4 teaspoons baking powder

1 teaspoon baking soda

1 teaspoon salt

1 cup dried cranberries

1 cup sliced almonds, toasted

1 egg, lightly beaten

1½ cups buttermilk, plus extra for brushing scones

2 teaspoons almond extract

Sugar and sliced almonds (optional)

Preheat oven to 425°F. In a large bowl, cut butter into flour, sugar, baking powder, baking soda, and salt until mixture resembles fine crumbs. Stir in cranberries and almonds. Add egg, buttermilk, and almond extract; mix until ingredients cling together and form soft dough. Turn dough onto a lightly floured surface and knead gently about 15 times. Divide dough equally into quarters and pat into ½-inch-thick circles. Cut each circle into 6 wedges. Place wedges on a lightly greased baking sheets. Brush scones lightly with buttermilk and sprinkle with sugar and a few sliced almonds, if desired. Bake for 12 to 15 minutes, or until scones are golden brown.

Joshua Grindle Inn
Mendocino, California

Dried Cherry Scones

Sixteen Scones

6 tablespoons cold butter

2 cups all-purpose flour

2 tablespoons granulated sugar

1 tablespoon baking powder

½ teaspoon salt

1 tablespoon finely grated orange zest

¾ cup dried cherries

1 egg, lightly beaten

½ cup milk

Glaze:

1 cup confectioners' sugar

1 to 2 tablespoons orange juice

1 teaspoon finely grated orange zest

Preheat oven to 400°F. In a large bowl, cut butter into flour, sugar, baking powder, and salt until mixture resembles fine crumbs. Stir in orange zest and cherries. Add egg and milk; mix until ingredients cling together and form soft dough. Turn dough onto a lightly floured surface and knead gently about 15 times. Divide dough into fourths and pat into squares about ½ inch thick. Cut each square diagonally twice to form 4 triangles. Place triangles on a lightly greased baking sheet (or freeze for future baking). Bake for about 15 minutes, or until scones are golden brown.

For glaze, in a small bowl, combine confectioners' sugar, orange juice, and orange zest to desired consistency. Spoon glaze over hot scones; let cool 5 minutes.

The Honor Mansion
Healdsburg, California

Date Pecan Scones

Eight Scones

4 tablespoons cold butter

2⅓ cups all-purpose flour

3 tablespoons brown sugar

1 tablespoon baking powder

½ teaspoon baking soda

½ teaspoon salt

½ cup chopped pitted dates

½ cup chopped pecans

1 egg, lightly beaten

¾ cup heavy (whipping) cream

1 teaspoon vanilla extract

Heavy (whipping) cream and granulated sugar (optional)

Preheat oven to 400°F. In a large bowl, cut butter into flour, brown sugar, baking powder, baking soda, and salt until mixture resembles fine crumbs. Stir in dates and pecans. Add egg, cream, and vanilla; mix until ingredients cling together and form soft dough. Turn dough onto a lightly floured surface and knead gently about 30 seconds. Pat dough into a ¾-inch-thick circle. Cut into 8 wedges. Place wedges on an ungreased baking sheet. Brush scones lightly with cream and sprinkle with sugar, if desired. Bake for 15 to 18 minutes, or until scones are golden brown.

Hartley House Bed & Breakfast Inn
Sacramento, California

Oatmeal Scones

Eight Scones

½ cup (1 stick) cold butter

1¼ cups all-purpose flour

⅓ cup packed brown sugar

1 teaspoon baking powder

½ teaspoon baking soda

½ teaspoon salt

1 cup old-fashioned oats

⅓ cup golden raisins

⅓ cup buttermilk

Preheat oven to 375°F. In a large bowl, cut butter into flour, brown sugar, baking powder, baking soda, and salt until mixture resembles fine crumbs; stir in oats and raisins. Add buttermilk and mix until ingredients cling together and form soft dough. Turn dough onto a lightly floured surface and pat into a 7-inch circle. Cut into 8 wedges. Place wedges on an ungreased baking sheet. Bake for 12 to 15 minutes, or until scones are golden brown.

The George Alexander House
Healdsburg, California

Berry-Filled Scones

Four Scones

1½ cups all-purpose flour

2 teaspoons cream of tartar

2 tablespoons sugar

1 teaspoon baking soda

3 tablespoons cold butter

½ cup milk

Whipped cream (optional)

Filling:

1 pint fresh or frozen blueberries (thawed, if frozen)

1 tablespoon cornstarch

1 tablespoon sugar

Fresh seasonal berries (raspberries, blackberries, etc.)

Preheat oven to 400°F. In a large bowl, combine flour, cream of tartar, sugar, and baking soda. Cut in butter until mixture is the consistency of coarse crumbs. Add milk; mix lightly until well blended. Pat into a ½-inch-thick circle; cut into fourths. Place scones on a lightly greased cookie sheet. Bake for 15 minutes, or until scones are golden brown.

For filling, combine blueberries, cornstarch, and sugar in a medium saucepan. Cook over medium heat until blueberries form a sauce. Add other berries and heat until warm. Split scones in half and fill with fruit. Top with whipped cream, if desired.

The Beech Tree Manor
Seattle, Washington

Orange Currant Scones

Sixteen Scones

2 cups all-purpose flour

2 tablespoons sugar

1 tablespoon baking powder

½ teaspoon salt

¾ cup dried currants

1 tablespoon finely grated orange zest

6 tablespoons cold butter

1 egg, lightly beaten

½ cup milk

Preheat oven to 400°F. In a large bowl, combine flour, sugar, baking powder, and salt. Stir in currants and orange zest. Cut in butter until mixture resembles fine crumbs. Add egg and milk. Mix until dough clings together. Turn dough onto a lightly floured surface and knead gently about 15 times. Divide dough into fourths and pat into squares about ½ inch thick. Cut each square diagonally twice to form 4 triangles. Place triangles on a lightly greased baking sheet (or freeze for future baking). Bake for 15 to 20 minutes, or until scones are golden brown.

The James House
Port Townsend, Washington

French Breakfast Puffs

Fifteen Puffs

⅓ cup shortening

½ cup sugar

1 egg

1½ cups all-purpose flour

1½ teaspoons baking powder

½ teaspoon salt

¼ teaspoon ground nutmeg

½ cup milk

½ cup (1 stick) butter, melted

Cinnamon sugar (½ cup sugar mixed with
   ½ teaspoon ground cinnamon)

Preheat oven to 350°F. In a large bowl, cream shortening, sugar, and egg. In a separate bowl, combine flour, baking powder, salt, and nutmeg. Add flour mixture to creamed mixture alternately with milk. Fill greased muffin tins two-thirds full. Bake for 20 to 25 minutes, or until puffs are golden brown. Remove puffs from oven and immediately roll in butter and then in cinnamon sugar.

Abigail's
Victoria, British Columbia

Fresh Blueberry Muffins

Twelve Muffins

3 cups all-purpose flour

½ cup granulated sugar

1½ tablespoons baking powder

½ teaspoon salt

¾ cup fresh or frozen blueberries

3 eggs

1½ cups milk

⅓ cup vegetable oil

Topping:

½ cup packed brown sugar

½ cup chopped walnuts

1 teaspoon ground cinnamon

Preheat oven to 400°F. In a large bowl, combine flour, sugar, baking powder, and salt. Stir in blueberries. In a separate bowl, beat eggs; add milk and oil. Mix well and add to dry mixture. Fold gently just until moistened. Fill greased muffin tins two-thirds full.

For topping, in a small bowl combine brown sugar, walnuts, and cinnamon. Sprinkle each muffin with 1 tablespoon of topping. Bake for 20 minutes, or until a toothpick inserted into center of muffins comes out clean.

San Juan Inn
Friday Harbor, Washington

Apricot Cornmeal Muffins

Thirty Muffins

1¼ cups (2½ sticks) butter, softened

2 cups sugar

5 eggs

1 teaspoon vanilla extract

4 cups buttermilk

5 cups all-purpose flour

1 cup cornmeal

1½ tablespoons baking powder

1½ tablespoons baking soda

3 cups finely chopped dried apricots

Preheat oven to 350°F. In a large bowl, cream butter and sugar with an electric mixer; add eggs and vanilla. With mixer running slowly, add buttermilk (do not overmix). Add flour, cornmeal, baking powder, and baking soda; mix just until combined (batter will be lumpy). Fold in apricots. Fill greased muffin cups two-thirds full. Bake for 20 to 25 minutes, or until a toothpick inserted into center of muffins comes out clean.

Columbia City Hotel
Columbia, California

Raspberry Streusel Muffins

Twelve Muffins

1½ cups all-purpose flour

¼ cup granulated sugar

¼ cup packed brown sugar

2 teaspoons baking powder

¼ teaspoon ground cinnamon

1 egg, lightly beaten

½ cup milk

½ cup (1 stick) butter, melted

1¼ cups fresh or frozen raspberries (if frozen, mix with
    2 tablespoons flour)

Topping:

½ cup chopped nuts

½ cup packed brown sugar

¼ cup all-purpose flour

2 teaspoons grated orange zest

1 teaspoon ground cinnamon

Preheat oven to 350°F. In a large bowl, combine flour, sugars, baking powder, and cinnamon. Make a well in center and add egg, milk, and butter. Mix with a wooden spoon just until blended, being careful not to overmix. Gently fold in raspberries. Fill greased muffin tins two-thirds full.

For topping, in a small bowl combine nuts, brown sugar, flour, orange zest, and cinnamon. Sprinkle each muffin tin with 1 tablespoon of topping. Bake for 20 to 25 minutes, or until a toothpick inserted into center of muffins comes out clean.

Eagles Nest Inn
Langley, Washington

Oatmeal Peach Muffins

Twelve Muffins

1¼ cups all-purpose flour

1 cup old-fashioned oats

¼ cup packed brown sugar

1½ teaspoons ground cinnamon

1 teaspoon baking soda

1 teaspoon baking powder

1 cup buttermilk

½ cup vegetable oil

2 tablespoons molasses

1 egg

1 teaspoon vanilla extract

¾ cup chopped walnuts

1 cup peeled and chopped fresh peaches

Preheat oven to 400°F. In a large bowl, combine flour, oats, brown sugar, cinnamon, baking soda, and baking powder. In a medium bowl, combine buttermilk, oil, molasses, egg, and vanilla. Add wet mixture to dry mixture and mix just until blended (batter will be lumpy). Stir in walnuts and peaches. Fill greased muffin tins two-thirds full. Bake for 20 minutes, or until a toothpick inserted into center of muffins comes out clean.

Galer Place
Seattle, Washington

Applesauce Walnut Muffins

Twelve Muffins

½ cup (1 stick) butter, softened

½ cup sugar

2 eggs

¾ cup applesauce

1¾ cups all-purpose flour

1 teaspoon baking soda

½ cup finely chopped walnuts

½ cup raisins

1 tablespoon flaked or shredded coconut

½ teaspoon salt

Preheat oven to 400°F. In a large bowl, cream butter and sugar until fluffy. Beat in eggs until light. Add applesauce. In a separate bowl, stir together flour, baking soda, walnuts, raisins, coconut, and salt. Add flour mixture to applesauce mixture, mixing just until blended. Fill greased muffin tins two-thirds full. Bake for 15 minutes, or until a toothpick inserted into center of muffins comes out clean.

Glenacres Inn
Westport, Washington

Orange Apricot Muffins

Twelve Muffins

2 cups all-purpose flour

⅔ cup sugar

1 tablespoon baking powder

¼ teaspoon salt

1 egg, lightly beaten

⅓ cup butter, melted

¾ cup orange juice

½ cup milk

1 tablespoon grated orange zest

1 cup chopped nuts

1 cup chopped dried apricots

Preheat oven to 400°F. In a large bowl, sift together flour, sugar, baking powder, and salt; set aside. In a separate bowl, combine egg, butter, orange juice, milk, orange zest, nuts, and apricots. Add flour mixture, and mix just until blended. Fill greased muffin tins two-thirds full. Bake for 20 minutes, or until a toothpick inserted into center of muffins comes out clean.

Roberta's Bed & Breakfast
Seattle, Washington

Low-Fat Yogurt Muffins

Twelve Muffins

1 cup all-purpose flour (use half whole wheat flour, if desired)

1 cup wheat germ

4 teaspoons baking powder

½ teaspoon salt

¼ teaspoon baking soda

2 tablespoons butter

1 cup packed brown sugar

1 egg

1 teaspoon grated orange zest

¼ cup orange juice

¾ cup plain yogurt

Preheat oven to 425°F. In a medium bowl, combine flour, wheat germ, baking powder, salt, and baking soda. In a large bowl, cream together butter, brown sugar, and egg; add orange zest and juice, and yogurt. Add dry mixture, and mix just until blended. Fill greased muffin tins two-thirds full. Bake for 15 to 18 minutes, or until a toothpick inserted into center of muffins comes out clean.

Top O' Triangle Mountain
Victoria, British Columbia

Banana–Oat Bran Muffins

Twelve Muffins

1 egg

¾ cup packed light brown sugar

1⅓ cups (about 3) ripe bananas, mashed

1 cup raisins or walnuts

⅓ cup vegetable oil

1 teaspoon vanilla extract

¼ cup molasses

½ cup flaked or shredded coconut

¾ cup all-purpose flour

¾ cup whole wheat flour

½ cup oat bran

2 teaspoons baking powder

½ teaspoon baking soda

1 teaspoon ground cinnamon

¼ teaspoon salt

Preheat oven to 375°F. In a medium bowl, whisk together egg and brown sugar. Beat in bananas, raisins, oil, vanilla, molasses, and coconut. In a separate bowl, combine flours, oat bran, baking powder, baking soda, cinnamon, and salt. Using a spatula, gently fold in banana mixture just until blended. Fill greased muffin tins two-thirds full. Bake for 20 minutes, or until muffins are golden brown.

Lake Chelan River House
Chelan, Washington

Gingerbread Muffins

Twenty-Four Muffins

½ cup shortening

½ cup (1 stick) margarine

1 cup sugar

1 cup dark molasses

4 eggs

2 teaspoons baking soda

1 cup buttermilk

4 cups all-purpose flour

2 teaspoons ground ginger

½ teaspoon ground cinnamon

½ teaspoon ground cloves

½ teaspoon ground allspice

1 cup sour cream

1 cup raisins

1 cup chopped pecans, toasted

Preheat oven to 350°F. In a large bowl, cream shortening, margarine, sugar, and molasses. Add eggs, one at a time, beating well after each. In a small bowl, dissolve baking soda in buttermilk. In a separate bowl, combine flour, ginger, cinnamon, cloves, and allspice. Add flour mixture alternately with buttermilk mixture to creamed mixture. Fold in sour cream, raisins, and pecans. Fill greased muffin cups two-thirds full. Bake for 20 to 25 minutes, or until a toothpick inserted into center of muffins comes out clean. (*Note:* This batter can be stored in a covered airtight container in the refrigerator up to two weeks.)

The Carriage House
Laguna Beach, California

Mini Lemon Muffins

Eighteen Mini Muffins

½ cup (1 stick) butter, softened

½ cup sugar

Grated zest of 1 lemon

2 eggs, separated

1 cup all-purpose flour

1 teaspoon baking powder

¼ teaspoon salt

¼ cup lemon juice

Preheat oven to 400°F. In a large bowl, cream butter, sugar, and lemon zest. Add egg yolks and beat well. In a medium bowl, combine flour, baking powder, and salt. Add flour mixture alternately with lemon juice to creamed mixture, mixing well after each addition. In a separate bowl, beat egg whites until stiff; fold into batter. Fill greased mini muffin cups two-thirds full. Bake for 12 to 15 minutes, or until muffins are golden brown.

Meadow Creek Ranch Bed & Breakfast
Mariposa, California

Ginger Pear Muffins

Twelve Muffins

2 eggs

2 teaspoons milk

½ cup vegetable oil

¾ cup sugar

2 cups all-purpose flour

2 teaspoons baking powder

½ teaspoon salt

½ teaspoon ground cardamom

1 tablespoon finely chopped crystallized ginger

2 medium pears, peeled and finely chopped

¾ cup chopped walnuts

½ cup raisins

Preheat oven to 350°F. In a large bowl, beat eggs, milk, oil, and sugar. Stir in flour, baking powder, salt, cardamom, and ginger; mix just until blended. Fold in pears, walnuts, and raisins. Fill greased muffin cups two-thirds full. Bake for 20 to 25 minutes, or until a toothpick inserted into center of muffins comes out clean.

Coast Guard House Historic Inn
Point Arena, California

Apple Cranberry Muffins

Twelve Muffins

2 eggs

1 cup milk

½ cup vegetable oil

1 cup sugar

3 cups all-purpose flour

4 teaspoons baking powder

1 teaspoon salt

1½ teaspoons ground cinnamon

1 cup dried cranberries

½ cup golden raisins

2 small cooking apples, peeled and chopped

Cinnamon sugar (¼ cup sugar mixed with
   ¾ teaspoon ground cinnamon)

Preheat oven to 400°F. In a large bowl, beat eggs, milk, oil, and sugar. Stir in flour, baking powder, salt, and cinnamon; mix just until blended (batter will be thick). Fold in cranberries, raisins, and apples. Fill greased muffin cups two-thirds full. Sprinkle muffins with cinnamon sugar. Bake for 20 to 25 minutes, or until a toothpick inserted into center of muffins comes out clean.

Captain's Cove Inn
Mendocino, California

Pumpkin Pie Muffins

Twelve Muffins

2 eggs

¼ cup buttermilk

½ cup (1 stick) butter, melted

3 tablespoons molasses

¾ cup canned pumpkin

1 teaspoon vanilla extract

2 cups all-purpose flour

¾ cup packed brown sugar

1½ teaspoons baking powder

¼ teaspoon baking soda

¾ cup coarsely chopped pecans or walnuts

¾ cup chopped pitted dates

Preheat oven to 400°F. In a large bowl, beat eggs, buttermilk, butter, molasses, pumpkin, and vanilla. Stir in flour, brown sugar, baking powder, and baking soda; mix just until blended. Fold in pecans and dates. Fill greased muffin cups two-thirds full. Bake for 20 to 25 minutes, or until a toothpick inserted into center of muffins comes out clean.

The Zaballa House Bed & Breakfast
Half Moon Bay, California

Mandarin Orange Muffins

Twelve Muffins

BREAKFAST
IN BED

1 can (11 ounces) mandarin orange segments

1 tablespoon orange extract

1 egg

1 cup sour cream

½ cup (1 stick) butter, melted

½ cup granulated sugar

½ cup packed brown sugar

2 cups all-purpose flour

2 teaspoons baking powder

½ teaspoon baking soda

½ teaspoon salt

½ cup chopped pecans

Preheat oven to 400°F. Drain oranges; reserve liquid. Cut oranges in half and place in a measuring cup. Add orange extract and reserved liquid to equal 1 cup. In a large bowl, beat egg, sour cream, butter, and sugars; stir in orange mixture. Add flour, baking powder, baking soda, and salt; mix just until blended. Fold in pecans. Fill greased muffin cups two-thirds full. Bake for 20 to 25 minutes, or until a toothpick inserted into center of muffins comes out clean.

Orchard Hill Country Inn
Julian, California

Cran-Blackberry Muffins

Twelve Muffins

1 egg

¾ cup milk

½ cup vegetable oil

⅓ cup sugar

2 cups all-purpose flour

1 tablespoon baking powder

1 teaspoon salt

1 tablespoon grated lemon zest

¾ cup fresh or frozen blackberries

½ cup chopped fresh or frozen cranberries

½ cup chopped hazelnuts

Preheat oven to 400°F. In a large bowl, beat egg, milk, oil, and sugar. Stir in flour, baking powder, salt, and lemon zest; mix just until blended. Fold in blackberries, cranberries, and hazelnuts. Fill greased muffin cups two-thirds full. Bake for about 20 minutes, or until a toothpick inserted into center of muffins comes out clean.

The Daly Inn
Eureka, California

GLAZED CINNAMON BREAD

HONEY AND OATS BREAD

EYE-OPENER JALEPEÑO CORN BREAD

IRISH SODA BREAD

HAWAIIAN BREAKFAST BREAD

PUMPKIN GINGERBREAD

LEMON HUCKLEBERRY BREAD

STRAWBERRY NUT BREAD

PEAR ALMOND BREAD

APPLESAUCE RAISIN BREAD

BANANA PECAN BREAD

CRANBERRY NUT BREAD

RASPBERRY LEMON TEA BREAD

CHOCOLATE ZUCCHINI BREAD

RASPBERRY CREAM CHEESE COFFEE CAKE

SOUR CREAM PECAN COFFEE CAKE

BLUEBERRY CREAM CHEESE COFFEE CAKE

FRESH PLUM COFFEE CAKE

BLUEBERRY STREUSEL COFFEE CAKE

RHUBARB BUTTERMILK COFFEE CAKE

PUMPKIN CRANBERRY COFFEE CAKE

CHOCOLATE ZUCCHINI RUM CAKE

STICKY BREAD COFFEE CAKE

Breads &
Coffee Cakes

Glazed Cinnamon Bread

One Loaf

1 package active dry yeast

¼ cup warm water (105°F to 115°F)

⅔ cup warm milk (105°F to 115°F)

1 teaspoon salt

½ cup sugar, divided

½ cup (1 stick) butter, melted and cooled, divided

2 eggs

3 to 3½ cups all-purpose flour, divided, plus more for kneading

1½ teaspoons ground cinnamon

Icing:

½ cup confectioners' sugar

1 tablespoon milk

½ teaspoon vanilla extract

Preheat oven to 350°F. In a large bowl, combine yeast and water; let stand until bubbly. Stir in milk, salt, ¼ cup of the sugar, and ¼ cup of the butter. Add eggs and 1½ cups of the flour; beat until smooth. Beat in remaining flour until dough is smooth and elastic. Turn dough over in a greased bowl; cover and let rise in a warm place until doubled (about 1 hour). Turn dough out onto a floured board and knead lightly, adding flour as needed until dough no longer sticks to fingers. Roll out into a 9- by 18-inch rectangle. Brush with 2 tablespoons of the butter. In a small bowl, mix the remaining sugar with cinnamon; sprinkle over dough. Roll up tightly. Turn loaf over and pinch seam together to seal. Put loaf into a greased 9- by 5-inch loaf pan. Brush top with remaining butter. Cover and let rise until almost doubled (about 45 minutes). Bake for 30 to 35 minutes, or until loaf is golden brown and sounds hollow when tapped. Place on a cooling rack.

For icing, in a small bowl, stir together confectioners' sugar, milk, and vanilla. While bread is still warm, drizzle icing over top and let run down sides. Cool before slicing.

Tucker House
Friday Harbor, Washington

Honey and Oats Bread

One Loaf

½ cup old-fashioned oats

1 cup boiling water

2 tablespoons butter

¼ cup honey

1 package active dry yeast

¼ cup warm water (105°F to 115°F)

1 cup milk

2 teaspoons salt

5 cups bread flour (approximately)

Melted butter, for brushing top

Preheat oven to 350°F. In a small saucepan, cook oats in boiling water for 5 minutes. Add butter and honey. Cool to lukewarm. In a small bowl, dissolve yeast in the warm water. Transfer oat mixture to a large bowl, and add yeast mixture. Mix in milk and salt. Add flour gradually to make a soft dough. Knead lightly. Shape into a loaf and place in a well-greased 9- by 5-inch loaf pan. Cover and let rise until doubled in bulk. Bake for 40 to 45 minutes, or until loaf sounds hollow when tapped. Remove from oven, and brush top with melted butter.

Country Willows
Ashland, Oregon

Eye-Opener Jalepeño Corn Bread

One Large Pan

1 cup buttermilk

1 cup cornmeal

¼ cup corn oil

2 eggs

1 cup all-purpose flour

3 tablespoons sugar

1 teaspoon baking powder

½ teaspoon baking soda

1 can (8 ounces) creamed corn

1 can (4 ounces) diced jalapeños

1 cup shredded cheddar cheese

¼ cup shredded Monterey Jack cheese

Preheat oven to 375°F. In a large bowl, combine buttermilk and cornmeal; let stand 30 minutes. Stir in oil, eggs, flour, sugar, baking powder, baking soda, corn, jalapeños, and cheeses; mix well. Pour batter into a greased 13- by 9-inch baking pan. Bake for about 30 minutes, or until a toothpick inserted into center of bread comes out clean.

Mendocino Village Inn
Mendocino, California

Irish Soda Bread

One Round Loaf

2 cups all-purpose flour

1 teaspoon salt

¾ teaspoon baking powder

¼ teaspoon plus pinch baking soda

1 to 1¼ cups buttermilk

Preheat oven to 375°F. In a large bowl, combine flour, salt, baking powder, and baking soda. Stir in 1 cup of the buttermilk and mix well, adding more buttermilk as needed until dough pulls away from sides of bowl and forms a ball. Place dough on a floured surface and knead for 30 seconds. Shape into a round loaf. Place on a greased cookie sheet and, using a sharp knife, score a large X on top of the loaf. Bake for 45 minutes, or until loaf sounds hollow when tapped.

Gaslight Inn
Seattle, Washington

Hawaiian Breakfast Bread

Two Loaves

3 eggs

1 cup vegetable oil

2 cups sugar

2 teaspoons vanilla extract

2½ cups all-purpose flour

1 teaspoon baking soda

1 teaspoon ground cinnamon

1 can (8 ounces) crushed pineapple, drained

1 cup grated fresh coconut

2 cups grated carrots

Preheat oven to 350°F. In a large bowl, beat eggs, oil, sugar, and vanilla. Stir in flour, baking soda, and cinnamon; mix just until blended. Fold in pineapple, coconut, and carrots. Divide batter evenly into two greased 9- by 5-inch loaf pans and let rest 20 minutes. Bake for about 1 hour, or until a toothpick inserted into center of bread comes out clean. Cool completely. (*Note:* This bread cuts better the next day.)

Silver Rose Inn & Spa
Calistoga, California

Pumpkin Gingerbread

Two Loaves

BREAKFAST
IN BED

3 cups sugar

1 cup vegetable oil

4 eggs

⅔ cup water

1 can (16 ounces) pumpkin

2 teaspoons ground ginger

1 teaspoon ground cinnamon

1 teaspoon ground nutmeg

1 teaspoon ground cloves

1 teaspoon ground allspice

3½ cups all-purpose flour

2 teaspoons baking soda

1½ teaspoons salt

½ teaspoon baking powder

Preheat oven to 350°F. In a large bowl, mix together sugar, oil, and eggs; add water. Beat in pumpkin, ginger, cinnamon, nutmeg, cloves, and allspice. In a medium bowl, sift together flour, baking soda, salt, and baking powder; add to pumpkin mixture and mix just until blended. Pour batter into two greased 9- by 5-inch loaf pans. Bake for 1 hour, or until a toothpick inserted into center of bread comes out clean.

The Gingerbread Mansion
Ferndale, California

Lemon Huckleberry Bread

One Loaf

⅓ cup butter, softened

1 cup sugar

3 tablespoons lemon extract

2 eggs

1½ cups all-purpose flour

1 teaspoon baking powder

1 teaspoon salt

8 ounces lemon yogurt

1 cup fresh or frozen huckleberries

Glaze:

Juice of 1 lemon

½ cup sugar

Preheat oven to 350°F. Line bottom and sides of a greased 8- by 4-inch loaf pan with waxed paper. In a large bowl, cream together butter, sugar, and lemon extract. Beat in eggs. In a medium bowl, sift together flour, baking powder, and salt; add to creamed mixture alternately with yogurt. Fold in huckleberries. Pour batter into prepared pan and bake for 50 to 60 minutes, or until a toothpick inserted into center of bread comes out clean. Remove bread from pan while still warm, and cool on a rack.

For glaze, combine lemon juice with sugar; brush over top of warm loaf. (*Note:* This bread cuts better the next day.)

Mio Amore Pensione
Trout Lake, Washington

Strawberry Nut Bread

One Loaf

BREAKFAST
IN BED

2 eggs

½ cup vegetable oil

1 cup sugar

½ teaspoon vanilla extract

1½ cups all-purpose flour

½ teaspoon baking soda

½ teaspoon salt

1 cup milk

½ cup finely chopped walnuts

¾ cup chopped fresh strawberries

Preheat oven to 350°F. In a large bowl, beat eggs, oil, sugar, and vanilla. In a separate bowl, combine flour, baking soda, and salt. Add flour mixture alternately with milk to egg mixture. Fold in walnuts and strawberries. Pour batter into a greased 9- by 5-inch loaf pan. Bake for about 1 hour, or until a toothpick inserted into center of bread comes out clean.

The Inn San Francisco
San Francisco, California

Pear Almond Bread

Five Small Loaves

3 eggs

1 cup vegetable oil

1½ cups sugar

½ teaspoon grated lemon zest

1 teaspoon vanilla extract

3 Bartlett pears, peeled and chopped

3 cups unbleached flour

1 teaspoon salt

1 teaspoon baking soda

¼ teaspoon baking powder

1½ teaspoons ground cinnamon

Dash freshly ground nutmeg

⅔ cup chopped almonds

Preheat oven to 325°F. In a large bowl, beat eggs until light and fluffy. Add oil, sugar, zest, vanilla, and pears; mix well. In a separate bowl, sift together flour, salt, baking soda, baking powder, cinnamon, and nutmeg; add to pear mixture and mix just until blended. Fold in almonds. Pour batter into 5 greased miniature loaf pans. Bake for 35 to 40 minutes, or until a toothpick inserted into center of bread comes out clean.

Hersey House
Ashland, Oregon

Applesauce Raisin Bread

One Loaf

1 egg, beaten

1 cup applesauce

¼ cup (½ stick) butter, melted

½ cup granulated sugar

¼ cup packed brown sugar

1½ cups all-purpose flour

½ cup oat bran

2 teaspoons baking powder

¾ teaspoon salt

½ teaspoon baking soda

1 teaspoon ground nutmeg

½ teaspoon ground cinnamon

½ cup raisins

1 cup coarsely chopped walnuts

Preheat oven to 350°F. In a large bowl, mix together egg, applesauce, butter, and sugars. In a medium bowl, sift flour and combine with oat bran, baking powder, salt, baking soda, nutmeg, and cinnamon. Add to applesauce mixture, and mix until smooth. Fold in raisins and walnuts. Bake in a greased 9- by 5-inch loaf pan for 1 hour, or until a toothpick inserted into center of bread comes out clean.

Mountain Home Lodge
Leavenworth, Washington

Banana Pecan Bread

One Loaf

⅓ cup shortening

⅔ cup sugar

2 eggs

1 pound (3 to 4) ripe bananas, mashed

1¾ cups all-purpose flour

2¾ teaspoons baking powder

½ teaspoon salt

1 cup chopped pecans

Preheat oven to 350°F. In a large bowl, cream shortening. Add sugar and eggs; beat several minutes, until light and fluffy. Add bananas; blend well. In a medium bowl, sift together flour, baking powder, and salt; add to banana mixture. Fold in pecans. Turn batter into a greased 9- by 5-inch loaf pan. Bake for 60 to 70 minutes, or until a toothpick inserted into center of bread comes out clean. (*Note:* This bread keeps best when refrigerated.)

Westwinds Bed & Breakfast
Friday Harbor, Washington

Cranberry Nut Bread

One Loaf

2 tablespoons butter

1 egg

1 cup sugar

¾ cup orange juice

2 cups all-purpose flour

1 teaspoon baking powder

½ teaspoon baking soda

½ teaspoon salt

2 cups whole fresh cranberries

½ cup chopped nuts

Preheat oven to 350°F. In a large bowl, combine butter, egg, and sugar; mix well. Add orange juice, flour, baking powder, baking soda, and salt; stir just until moistened. Fold in cranberries and nuts. Bake in a greased 9- by 5-inch loaf pan for 60 to 70 minutes, or until a toothpick inserted into center of bread comes out clean.

White Sulphur Springs Ranch
Clio, California

Raspberry Lemon Tea Bread

Sixteen Servings

¾ cup (1½ sticks) butter, softened

2 cups sugar

4 eggs

¾ cup sour cream

½ cup milk

2 tablespoons grated lemon zest

⅓ cup lemon juice

3 cups all-purpose flour

2 teaspoons baking powder

1 cup fresh raspberries

Preheat oven to 325°F. In a large bowl, cream butter and sugar; add eggs, sour cream, milk, lemon zest, and lemon juice. Stir in flour and baking powder; mix just until blended. Fold in raspberries. Pour batter into greased 10-inch fluted tube pan. Bake for about 1 hour, or until a toothpick inserted into center of bread comes out clean. Cool before slicing.

Inn at Playa del Rey
Playa del Rey, California

Chocolate Zucchini Bread

Two Loaves

3 eggs

1 cup vegetable oil

2 teaspoons vanilla extract

2 cups sugar

3 cups grated zucchini

2⅓ cups all-purpose flour

½ cup unsweetened cocoa

2 teaspoons baking soda

1 teaspoon ground cinnamon

1 teaspoon salt

¼ teaspoon baking powder

½ cup chopped nuts

½ cup chocolate chips

Preheat oven to 350°F. In a medium bowl, mix together eggs, oil, vanilla, sugar, and zucchini. In a large bowl, combine flour, cocoa, baking soda, cinnamon, salt, and baking powder; stir in nuts and chocolate chips. Add zucchini mixture to flour mixture. Pour batter into 2 greased 9- by 5-inch loaf pans. Bake for 45 minutes, or until a toothpick inserted into center of bread comes out clean.

The Victorian Bed & Breakfast
Coupeville, Washington

Raspberry Cream Cheese Coffee Cake

Twelve Servings

2½ cups all-purpose flour

¾ cup sugar

¾ cup (1½ sticks) cold butter

½ teaspoon baking powder

½ teaspoon baking soda

¼ teaspoon salt

¾ cup sour cream

1 egg, lightly beaten

1 teaspoon almond extract

Filling:

8 ounces cream cheese

¼ cup sugar

1 egg, lightly beaten

½ cup raspberry jam

Topping:

½ cup sliced almonds

Preheat oven to 350°F. In a large bowl, combine flour and sugar; cut in butter until mixture resembles coarse crumbs. Remove 1 cup of crumbs for topping; reserve. To remaining crumb mixture in bowl, add baking powder, baking soda, salt, sour cream, egg, and almond extract; mix well. Spread batter in a greased and floured 9-inch springform pan.

For filling, in a small bowl, combine cream cheese, sugar, and egg; spread evenly over batter in pan. Spoon jam evenly over the cheese filling.

For topping, in a small bowl, combine reserved crumbs with almonds; sprinkle over jam. Bake for 1 hour, or until cream cheese is set and crust is deep golden brown. Cool 15 minutes; remove sides of pan and cool completely.

Campbell Ranch Inn
Geyserville, California

Sour Cream Pecan Coffee Cake

Twelve Servings

1 cup (2 sticks) butter, softened

2 cups sugar

2 eggs

2 cups sour cream

1 tablespoon vanilla extract

1 cup whole wheat flour

1 cup all-purpose flour

1 tablespoon baking powder

¼ teaspoon salt

Filling:

2 cups finely chopped pecans

½ cup sugar

1½ teaspoons ground cinnamon

Preheat oven to 350°F. In a large bowl, cream butter and sugar; add eggs, sour cream, and vanilla. Stir in flours, baking powder, and salt; mix well. Pour half of batter into a greased and floured 10-inch fluted tube pan.

For filling, in a small bowl, combine pecans, sugar, and cinnamon; sprinkle half of filling over batter. Top with remaining batter and then sprinkle with remaining filling mixture. Bake for about 1 hour, or until a toothpick inserted into center of cake comes out clean.

Four Sisters Inns
Monterey, California

Blueberry Cream Cheese Coffee Cake

Sixteen Servings

1½ cups sugar

3 cups all-purpose flour

4 teaspoons baking powder

1 teaspoon salt

8 ounces cream cheese, cut into ½-inch cubes

1½ cups fresh or frozen blueberries

3 eggs

½ cup sour cream

⅔ cup milk

½ cup (1 stick) butter, melted

1 cup chopped walnuts

Preheat oven to 350°F. In a large bowl, combine sugar, flour, baking powder, and salt. Toss cream cheese and blueberries in flour mixture to coat. In a separate bowl, beat eggs, sour cream, milk, and butter. Stir egg mixture into flour mixture; mix just until combined. Spread batter in a greased 13- by 9-inch baking pan; sprinkle with walnuts. Bake for 55 to 60 minutes, or until a toothpick inserted into center of cake comes out clean.

Apple Lane Inn
Aptos, California

Fresh Plum Coffee Cake

Eighteen Servings

2 eggs

1 cup milk

½ cup vegetable oil

1½ cups granulated sugar

3 cups all-purpose flour

1 tablespoon baking powder

1 teaspoon salt

6 to 8 plums, pitted and sliced

Topping:

6 tablespoons butter

1 cup packed brown sugar

6 tablespoons all-purpose flour

1½ teaspoons ground cinnamon

1 cup chopped walnuts

Preheat oven to 350°F. In a large bowl, beat eggs, milk, oil, and sugar. Stir in flour, baking powder, and salt; mix well. Spread batter in a greased and floured 13- by 9-inch glass baking dish. Top with rows of plum slices.

For topping, in a medium bowl, combine butter, brown sugar, flour, cinnamon, and walnuts; mix until crumbly and sprinkle over plums. Bake for about 1 hour, or until a toothpick inserted into center of cake comes out clean.

Old Thyme Inn
Half Moon Bay, California

Blueberry Streusel Coffee Cake

Nine Servings

2 cups all-purpose flour

¾ cup sugar

2½ teaspoons baking powder

½ teaspoon salt

¼ cup (½ stick) butter

¾ cup milk

1 egg

2 cups fresh or frozen blueberries

Topping:

½ cup sugar

⅓ cup all-purpose flour

½ teaspoon ground cinnamon

¼ teaspoon ground nutmeg

¼ cup (½ stick) butter, softened

Preheat oven to 375°F. In a large bowl, beat flour, sugar, baking powder, salt, butter, milk, and egg with an electric mixer on high speed for 30 seconds. Fold blueberries into batter. Pour batter into a greased 9-inch square cake pan.

For topping, in a medium bowl, combine sugar, flour, cinnamon, nutmeg, and butter; sprinkle over batter. Bake for 45 to 50 minutes, or until a toothpick inserted into center of cake comes out clean.

Amy's Manor Bed & Breakfast
Pateros, Washington

Rhubarb Buttermilk Coffee Cake

Twelve Servings

½ cup (1 stick) butter, softened

1 cup packed brown sugar

1 egg

1 teaspoon vanilla extract

2 cups all-purpose flour

1 teaspoon baking soda

½ teaspoon salt

1 cup buttermilk

2 cups fresh rhubarb, cut into ¼-inch pieces

Topping:

2 tablespoons butter, melted

½ cup packed brown sugar

1 teaspoon ground cinnamon

½ cup chopped walnuts or almonds

Preheat oven to 350°F. In a large bowl, cream butter and brown sugar; add egg and vanilla. In a separate bowl, mix flour, baking soda, and salt. Add flour mixture to creamed mixture alternately with buttermilk. Fold in rhubarb. Pour batter into a greased 13- by 9-inch baking pan.

For topping, in a small bowl, combine butter, brown sugar, cinnamon, and walnuts; sprinkle evenly over batter. Bake for 45 to 50 minutes, or until a toothpick inserted into center of cake comes out clean.

The Palm Hotel Bed & Breakfast
Jamestown, California

Pumpkin Cranberry Coffee Cake

Twelve Servings

2 eggs

½ cup vegetable oil

2 cups granulated sugar

1 cup canned pumpkin

2¼ cups all-purpose flour

1 teaspoon baking soda

½ teaspoon salt

1 tablespoon pumpkin pie spice

1 cup chopped fresh cranberries

Confectioners' sugar (optional)

Preheat oven to 350°F. In a large bowl, beat eggs, oil, sugar, and pumpkin. Stir in flour, baking soda, salt, and pumpkin pie spice; mix just until combined. Fold in cranberries. Spread batter evenly in a greased 8-cup ring mold. Place mold on a baking sheet. Bake for about 50 minutes, or until a toothpick inserted into center of cake comes out clean. Cool mold 10 minutes on a wire rack. Run knife around edge of cake to loosen and remove from mold. Dust with confectioners' sugar, if desired.

The Chichester-McKee House
Placerville, California

Chocolate Zucchini Rum Cake

Sixteen Servings

¾ cup (1½ sticks) butter, softened

2 cups granulated sugar

3 eggs

2 cups lightly packed shredded zucchini

⅓ cup rum, brandy, or water

¼ cup milk

2½ cups all-purpose flour

½ cup unsweetened cocoa

2½ teaspoons baking powder

1½ teaspoons baking soda

1 teaspoon salt

¾ teaspoon ground cinnamon

1 cup chopped walnuts

Glaze:

1⅔ cups confectioners' sugar

3 tablespoons rum or water

Preheat oven to 350°F. In a large bowl, beat butter and sugar with electric mixer until smooth. Beat in eggs, one at a time, until fluffy. Stir in zucchini, rum, and milk. Add flour, cocoa, baking powder, baking soda, salt, and cinnamon; mix well. Fold in walnuts. Spread batter in a greased and floured 10-inch fluted tube pan. Bake for 50 to 55 minutes, or until cake springs back when firmly pressed in center. Let cool in pan 15 minutes. Invert onto a rack and let cool.

For glaze, mix confectioners' sugar and rum; drizzle over cake.

Hammons House Inn Bed & Breakfast
Sonora, California

Sticky Bread Coffee Cake

Nine Servings

1 cup packed brown sugar

1 egg

¼ cup water

1 teaspoon baking soda

1 teaspoon ground cinnamon

⅛ teaspoon crushed whole cloves

½ cup raisins

1 loaf frozen bread dough, thawed

Preheat oven to 350°F. In a large bowl, combine brown sugar, egg, water, baking soda, cinnamon, and cloves. Fold in raisins. Tear bread dough into 1-inch cubes and toss with brown sugar mixture. Pour batter into a greased 9-inch square cake pan. Bake for 25 to 30 minutes, or until cake is golden brown.

Tucker's Bed & Breakfast
Victoria, British Columbia

OATMEAL BUTTERMILK PANCAKES

BANANA BUCKWHEAT PANCAKES

APPLE WALNUT PANCAKES

FLUFFY BLUEBERRY PANCAKES

RICOTTA PANCAKES

EASY ALMOND PANCAKES

APFEL PFANNKUCHEN

BLUE CORN PANCAKES WITH PINEAPPLE SALSA

SWEDISH PANCAKES WITH HUCKLEBERRY SAUCE

CINNAMON APPLE CREPES

FRESH FRUIT CREPES

HAZELNUT WAFFLES WITH PEACHES

CORNMEAL AND OAT WAFFLES

PUMPKIN SPICE WAFFLES

WILD RICE BELGIAN WAFFLES

WHOLE WHEAT WAFFLES

BUCKWHEAT BUTTERMILK WAFFLES

LEMON POPPY SEED FRENCH TOAST

PINEAPPLE FRENCH TOAST

APPLE PECAN FRENCH TOAST

ORANGE MARNIER FRENCH TOAST

SURPRISE STUFFED FRENCH TOAST

OVERNIGHT FRENCH TOAST

DECADENT CROISSANT FRENCH TOAST

PORTUGUESE PEACH FRENCH TOAST

Pancakes, Waffles & French Toast

Oatmeal Buttermilk Pancakes

Fourteen Pancakes

2 cups buttermilk

2 cups old-fashioned oats

2 eggs, lightly beaten

¼ cup (½ stick) butter, melted

1 teaspoon vanilla extract

½ cup all-purpose flour

2 tablespoons sugar

1 teaspoon baking powder

1 teaspoon baking soda

¼ teaspoon salt

½ teaspoon ground cinnamon

½ cup currants

In a large bowl, combine buttermilk and oats; let soak 30 minutes or overnight. Add eggs, butter, vanilla, flour, sugar, baking powder, baking soda, salt, cinnamon, and currants; mix well.

Heat a griddle or skillet over medium heat and grease if necessary. Pour ¼ cup batter for each pancake onto hot griddle. Cook pancakes until puffed and dry around edges. Flip and cook other side until pancakes are golden brown.

Lost Whale Inn
Trinidad, California

Banana Buckwheat Pancakes

Thirty-Six Pancakes

1 cup all-purpose flour

1 cup whole wheat flour

1 cup buckwheat flour

3 tablespoons sugar

2 tablespoons baking powder

1½ teaspoons baking soda

¾ teaspoon salt

3 eggs

6 tablespoons vegetable oil

3 cups buttermilk

3 ripe bananas, mashed

In a large bowl, combine flours, sugar, baking powder, baking soda, and salt. In a separate bowl, beat eggs, oil, and buttermilk; add bananas. Add egg mixture to flour mixture, and stir to combine.

Heat a griddle or skillet over medium heat and grease if necessary. Pour ¼ cup batter for each pancake onto hot griddle. Flip when bubbles form on surface; cook other side until pancakes are golden brown.

Ten Inverness Way
Inverness, California

Apple Walnut Pancakes

Ten to Twelve Pancakes

⅔ cup milk

2 tablespoons butter, melted

2 tablespoons molasses

1 egg

⅔ cup all-purpose flour

⅓ cup whole wheat flour

2 teaspoons baking powder

¼ teaspoon salt

¼ cup chopped walnuts

½ green apple, peeled and diced

In a large bowl, lightly beat together milk, butter, molasses, and egg. In a separate bowl, sift together flours, baking powder, and salt. Add walnuts and apple to flour mixture; add to milk mixture, and mix just until blended. If necessary, add additional milk to make batter the consistency of whipping cream.

Heat a griddle or skillet over medium heat and grease if necessary. Pour ¼ cup batter for each pancake onto hot griddle. Flip when bubbles form on surface; cook other side until pancakes are golden brown.

Mount Ashland Inn
Ashland, Oregon

Fluffy Blueberry Pancakes

Twelve Pancakes

1 egg

½ cup plain yogurt

½ cup milk

2 tablespoons vegetable oil

1 cup all-purpose flour

1 tablespoon sugar

1 teaspoon baking powder

1 teaspoon baking soda

¼ teaspoon salt

⅛ teaspoon ground nutmeg

¾ cup fresh or frozen blueberries (thawed, if frozen)

In a large bowl, beat egg, yogurt, milk, and oil. Stir in flour, sugar, baking powder, baking soda, salt, and nutmeg; mix just until blended (batter may be slightly lumpy).

Heat a griddle or skillet over medium heat and grease if necessary. Pour ¼ cup batter for each pancake onto hot griddle. Sprinkle pancakes with blueberries. Flip when bubbles form on surface; cook other side until pancakes are golden brown.

White Horse Inn Bed & Breakfast
Mammoth Lakes, California

Ricotta Pancakes

Sixteen Pancakes

3 eggs, separated

1 cup ricotta cheese

⅔ cup milk

½ cup all-purpose flour

1 teaspoon baking powder

½ teaspoon salt

Sour cream and jam, or whipped cream and fresh berries (optional)

In a large bowl, beat egg yolks, cheese, milk, flour, baking powder, and salt. In a separate bowl, beat egg whites until stiff. Gently fold egg whites into cheese mixture.

Heat a griddle or skillet over medium heat and grease if necessary. Pour ¼ cup batter for each pancake onto hot griddle. Cook pancakes until puffed and dry around edges. Flip and cook other side until pancakes are golden brown. Serve with sour cream and jam, or whipped cream and fresh berries, if desired.

The Gables Bed & Breakfast Inn
Santa Rosa, California

Easy Almond Pancakes

Eighteen Pancakes

4 cups buttermilk pancake mix

3 cups water

1 teaspoon almond extract

½ cup sliced almonds

Maple syrup and almond extract

In a large bowl, stir together pancake mix, water, and almond extract. Add more water if thinner pancakes are desired. Beat until smooth. (There will be some small lumps.) Fold in almonds.

Heat a griddle or skillet over medium heat and grease if necessary. Pour ⅓ cup batter for each pancake onto hot griddle. Flip when bubbles form on surface; cook other side until pancakes are golden brown. Serve with maple syrup heated with a few drops of almond extract, if desired.

Bennett House Bed & Breakfast
Port Angeles, Washington

Apfel Pfannkuchen

Sixteen Pancakes

5 eggs

½ cup water

1 teaspoon vanilla extract

1 teaspoon ground cinnamon

1½ cups buttermilk pancake mix

Butter for frying

3 apples, peeled and thinly sliced

In a large bowl, beat eggs, water, vanilla, and cinnamon until well blended. Add pancake mix; mix just until blended.

Heat a skillet over medium heat; melt 2 tablespoons butter in hot skillet. Ladle batter to make 3-inch pancakes. Immediately place apple slices on top of batter to cover entire pancake. Cook pancakes until golden brown and bubbly. Flip pancakes (adding butter if necessary) and cook other side until golden brown and crusty. Serve pancakes apple-side up.

Boulder Creek Bed & Breakfast
Yosemite-Mariposa, California

Blue Corn Pancakes with Pineapple Salsa

Twelve Pancakes

Pineapple Salsa:

1 fresh whole pineapple

1 cup corn syrup

½ cup dried currants

½ cup dried cherries

Juice and grated zest of 1 lime

Pancakes:

1 cup blue cornmeal

2 tablespoons sugar

½ teaspoon salt

1 cup boiling water

1 egg

¾ cup milk

2 tablespoons butter, melted

½ cup all-purpose flour

2 teaspoons baking powder

For salsa, cut pineapple into small chunks. Place in a medium bowl along with any juice extracted from cutting. Add corn syrup, currants, cherries, lime juice, and lime zest; mix well. Set aside.

For pancakes, in a large bowl, stir together cornmeal, sugar, salt, and boiling water. Let sit 10 minutes. In a separate bowl, beat together egg, milk, and butter; add to cornmeal mixture. In a small bowl, sift flour and baking powder; add to batter and mix well. Heat a griddle or skillet over medium heat and grease if necessary. Pour ¼ cup batter for each pancake onto hot griddle. Flip when bubbles form on surface; cook other side until pancakes are golden brown. Serve with pineapple salsa.

Rancho Caymus Inn
Rutherford, California

Swedish Pancakes with Huckleberry Sauce

Eight Pancakes

Huckleberry Sauce:

½ cup sugar

1½ tablespoons cornstarch

2 cups huckleberries

⅓ cup water

2 tablespoons lemon juice

Pancakes:

2 eggs, beaten

1 cup milk

1 cup all-purpose flour

1 teaspoon sugar

¼ teaspoon salt

⅓ cup butter

For sauce, combine sugar and cornstarch in a medium saucepan; stir in huckleberries. Add water and lemon juice. Cook over medium heat until thickened. Set aside.

For pancakes, in a medium bowl, combine eggs, milk, flour, sugar, and salt; beat until smooth. Melt butter over medium heat in a 8- or 9-inch cast-iron skillet; add to batter. Increase heat to medium-high, and pour ¼ cup batter for each pancake into skillet. Turn to coat bottom of skillet. Flip to brown both sides. Roll up pancake and keep warm in oven. Repeat with remaining batter. Serve with huckleberry sauce.

Waverly Place Bed & Breakfast
Spokane, Washington

Cinnamon Apple Crepes

Twelve Crepes

Cinnamon Apple Filling:

4 apples, peeled and sliced

2 tablespoons packed brown sugar

2 tablespoons butter

½ cup raisins

1 teaspoon ground cinnamon,

2 tablespoons amaretto liqueur

Crepes:

1½ cups milk

3 eggs

1¼ cups all-purpose flour

¼ teaspoon ground cinnamon, plus more for sprinkling

2 tablespoons butter, melted

For filling, in a large skillet, sauté apples and brown sugar in butter for 5 minutes. Add raisins, cinnamon, and liqueur; mix well. Remove from heat; set aside.

For crepes, combine milk, eggs, flour, and cinnamon in a blender. With motor running, add melted butter. Let sit at room temperature for 1 hour.

Heat an 8-inch nonstick skillet over medium-low heat. Pour ¼ cup batter for each crepe into skillet, allowing batter to spread evenly over bottom of pan. Cook crepe just until it begins to curl away from sides of pan, about 2 minutes. Flip and cook other side until golden brown. Transfer to a plate and repeat procedure with remaining batter. (*Note:* Crepes can be stored in refrigerator for up to 1 week.) Spoon ¼ cup cinnamon apple filling onto each warm crepe and roll crepe loosely. Sprinkle with cinnamon.

Foothill House
Calistoga, California

Fresh Fruit Crepes

Twelve Crepes

2 eggs

½ cup milk

½ cup water

1 cup all-purpose flour

¼ teaspoon salt

Sliced banana

Vanilla yogurt

Fresh mint sprigs

Fresh fruit (peaches, raspberries, blueberries, etc.)

Raspberry sauce or syrup

Confectioners' sugar (optional)

In a medium bowl, beat eggs, milk, and water. Stir in flour and salt to make thin batter. Let batter rest in refrigerator 1 hour.

Spray a 7-inch skillet with nonstick cooking spray; heat over medium-high heat. Pour ⅛ cup batter for each crepe into skillet; tilt pan to coat bottom evenly with a thin layer of batter. Cook crepe on one side only, just until it begins to curl away from sides of pan, or 1 to 2 minutes. Slide crepe onto plate and repeat with remaining batter, spraying pan as needed. Stack crepes on top of one another; cool.

To assemble crepes, place banana slices down center of crepe; top with a few spoonfuls of yogurt. Fold each side of crepe over center. Garnish with a dollop of yogurt and mint sprig. Surround with fresh fruit. Drizzle raspberry sauce in zigzag pattern over crepes. Lightly sift confectioners' sugar over entire plate, if desired.

Inn on Tomales Bay
Marshall, California

Hazelnut Waffles with Peaches

Six 7-Inch Waffles

1¼ cups milk

½ cup heavy (whipping) cream

¼ cup (½ stick) butter, softened

¼ cup sugar

Pinch salt

1¼ cups bread flour

1 tablespoon baking powder

3 eggs

¼ cup chopped hazelnuts

½ cup vanilla yogurt

Sliced fresh peaches

In a medium saucepan, heat milk, cream, butter, sugar, and salt over medium heat until sugar is dissolved; remove from stove. Pour milk mixture into a large bowl. Add flour and baking powder all at once; stir vigorously. Beat in eggs, one at a time, using an electric mixer. Fold in hazelnuts. (If batter is too runny or too thick, adjust with milk or flour as needed.) Let stand 5 minutes.

Heat a waffle iron and grease if necessary. Bake waffles in hot waffle iron until golden brown. Top each waffle with a dollop of yogurt and peaches.

Albion River Inn
Albion, California

Cornmeal and Oat Waffles

Six 7-Inch Waffles

2 eggs

1¾ cups buttermilk

¼ cup (½ stick) butter, melted

1 cup all-purpose flour

½ cup stone-ground yellow cornmeal

½ cup old-fashioned oats

2 teaspoons baking powder

In a large bowl, beat eggs, buttermilk, and butter. Add flour, cornmeal, oats, and baking powder; mix just until smooth (add more buttermilk to batter if too thick).

Heat a waffle iron and grease if necessary. Bake waffles in hot waffle iron until golden brown.

Carriage House Bed & Breakfast
Point Reyes, California

Pumpkin Spice Waffles

Six 4-Inch Waffles

3 eggs

1 cup milk

2 tablespoons butter, melted

2 tablespoons sugar

½ cup canned pumpkin

1 cup all-purpose flour

2 teaspoons baking powder

½ teaspoon salt

¼ teaspoon ground nutmeg

¼ teaspoon ground cloves

¼ teaspoon ground cinnamon

In a large bowl, beat eggs, milk, butter, sugar, and pumpkin. Add flour, baking powder, salt, nutmeg, cloves, and cinnamon; mix just until smooth.

Heat a waffle iron and grease if necessary. Bake waffles in hot waffle iron until golden brown.

Emma Nevada House
Nevada City, California

Wild Rice Belgian Waffles

Eight 4-Inch Waffles

4 eggs, separated

1⅓ cups milk

1 cup plain yogurt

⅓ cup vegetable oil

2 tablespoons honey

2 cups whole wheat flour

2½ teaspoons baking powder

¾ teaspoon baking soda

½ teaspoon salt

1½ cups cooked wild rice

1 cup chopped pecans, toasted

In a large bowl, beat egg yolks, milk, yogurt, oil, and honey. Stir in flour, baking powder, baking soda, and salt; mix just until blended. In a separate bowl, beat egg whites until stiff but not dry; gently fold into batter.

Heat a Belgian waffle iron and grease if necessary. Pour scant cupful of batter into center of hot waffle iron. Sprinkle 3 tablespoons of the wild rice and 2 tablespoons of the pecans over batter and bake until golden brown. Repeat for remaining batter.

Bears at the Beach Bed & Breakfast
San Diego, California

Whole Wheat Waffles

Four 7-Inch Waffles

2 cups whole wheat flour

2 teaspoons baking powder

3 eggs, separated

1½ cups whole milk

½ cup (1 stick) butter, melted

Fresh strawberries and whipped cream (optional)

In a large bowl, mix flour and baking powder; set aside. In a medium bowl, combine egg yolks, milk, and butter. In a separate bowl, beat egg whites until stiff. Add milk mixture to flour mixture; mix just until blended. Fold in egg whites.

Heat a waffle iron and grease if necessary. Bake waffles in hot waffle iron until golden brown. Serve with strawberries and whipped cream, if desired.

State Street Inn
Hood River, Oregon

Buckwheat Buttermilk Waffles

Four 7-Inch Waffles

¾ cup buckwheat flour

½ cup unbleached white flour

¼ cup whole wheat flour

2 teaspoons baking powder

¾ teaspoon baking soda

½ teaspoon salt

2 tablespoons sugar

3 eggs

1½ cups buttermilk

½ cup (1 stick) butter, melted and cooled

In a large bowl, combine flours, baking powder, baking soda, salt, and sugar. In a medium bowl, beat eggs, buttermilk, and butter. Add buttermilk mixture to flour mixture; mix just until blended.

Heat a waffle iron and grease if necessary. Bake waffles in hot waffle iron until golden brown.

Turtleback Farm Inn
Orcas Island, Washington

Lemon Poppy Seed French Toast

Six Servings

12 eggs

1¼ cups milk

Juice and zest of ½ lemon

1½ tablespoons poppy seeds

12 slices French bread, ¾ inch thick

¼ cup (½ stick) butter

Syrup:

1 cup maple syrup

¼ cup raisins

Juice and zest of ½ lemon

Lemon slices (optional)

In a large bowl, beat eggs, milk, lemon juice, lemon zest, and poppy seeds; pour into a large shallow pan. Soak bread slices in egg mixture for 30 minutes, turning once.

Heat a griddle or skillet over medium heat and grease if necessary. Cook bread on hot griddle until golden brown on both sides.

For syrup, in a small saucepan, heat maple syrup, raisins, lemon juice, and lemon zest over medium heat until warm. Serve syrup with French toast. Garnish with lemon slices, if desired.

Scott Courtyard
Calistoga, California

Pineapple French Toast

Six Servings

6 eggs

2 teaspoons vanilla extract

2 tablespoons sour cream

1 can (8 ounces) crushed pineapple, drained

½ cup half-and-half

2 tablespoons maple syrup

12 slices French bread, ¾ inch thick

Confectioners' sugar (optional)

Canned pineapple slices (optional)

In a blender, combine eggs, vanilla, sour cream, pineapple, half-and-half, and syrup; blend until smooth. Place bread in a large shallow pan; pour egg mixture over bread. Soak bread thoroughly, then turn to soak other side.

Heat a griddle or skillet over medium heat and grease if necessary. Cook bread on hot griddle until golden brown on both sides. Sprinkle with confectioners' sugar and garnish with pineapple, if desired.

Ben Maddox House
Visalia, California

Apple Pecan French Toast

Three Servings

¼ cup (½ stick) butter

3 Granny Smith apples, peeled and sliced

½ cup sugar

1 tablespoon ground cinnamon

5 eggs

¼ cup half-and-half

1 teaspoon vanilla extract

6 slices sweet French bread, ½ inch thick

2 teaspoons brandy

2 tablespoons chopped pecans

In a medium skillet, melt butter over medium heat; add apples, sugar, and cinnamon. Sauté apples until tender; keep warm. In a medium bowl, beat eggs, half-and-half, and vanilla; pour into a shallow bowl. Dip bread slices in egg mixture until thoroughly coated.

Heat a griddle or skillet over medium heat and grease if necessary. Cook bread on hot griddle until golden brown on both sides. Add brandy and pecans to apples; cook over medium-high heat for 30 seconds. Slice bread diagonally; top with apples and pecans.

Arbor House Inn
Lakeport, California

Orange Marnier French Toast

Six Servings

4 eggs plus 2 egg whites

½ cup sugar

¼ teaspoon salt

3 cups milk

1 tablespoon Grand Marnier liqueur

Grated zest of 1 orange

1 loaf sweet French bread, cut into twelve 1-inch-thick slices

Sprinkle of ground nutmeg

Confectioners' sugar

In a large bowl, whisk together eggs, egg whites, sugar, and salt. Stir in milk, liqueur, and orange zest; pour mixture into a shallow bowl. Soak bread in egg mixture until thoroughly saturated, about 1 minute. Arrange slices on a baking sheet and sprinkle lightly with nutmeg; let stand 1 hour (or refrigerate overnight).

Preheat oven to 400°F. Heat a griddle or skillet over medium heat and grease if necessary. Slowly brown both sides of bread, 2 to 3 minutes on each side. Place French toast on a clean baking sheet and bake for 20 minutes. Sprinkle generously with confectioners' sugar.

Brannan Cottage Inn
Calistoga, California

Surprise Stuffed French Toast

Six Servings

1 loaf day-old French bread, cut into twelve 1-inch-thick slices

¾ cup orange marmalade

4 eggs, lightly beaten

2 tablespoons milk

2 tablespoons triple sec liqueur

1 tablespoon maple syrup

1½ teaspoons grated orange zest

½ teaspoon ground nutmeg

Confectioners' sugar

Make a pocket slit in each slice of bread. Fill each pocket with 1 tablespoon of the marmalade. In a medium bowl, combine eggs, milk, liqueur, maple syrup, orange zest, and nutmeg; pour into a shallow dish. Soak bread in egg mixture until thoroughly saturated.

Heat a griddle or skillet over medium heat and grease if necessary. Cook bread for 2 to 5 minutes on each side, or until golden brown. Transfer to serving platter and sprinkle with confectioners' sugar.

Cedarym Bed & Breakfast
Redmond, Washington

Overnight French Toast

Four Servings

4 eggs

1 cup half-and-half

¼ cup sugar

8 slices French bread, ½ inch thick

¼ cup (½ stick) butter, for frying

6 fresh peaches, peeled and sliced

½ cup fresh raspberries

¼ cup sliced almonds, toasted

Confectioners' sugar or whipped cream (optional)

In a medium bowl, whisk together eggs, half-and-half, and sugar. Place bread slices in a shallow pan and pour egg mixture over top. Turn bread over to saturate thoroughly. Cover and refrigerate overnight.

Heat a griddle or skillet over medium heat and melt butter on hot griddle. Cook bread for 4 to 5 minutes on each side, or until golden brown. Top with peaches, raspberries, and almonds. Sprinkle with confectioners' sugar or top with a dollop of whipped cream, if desired.

The Morical House
Ashland, Oregon

Decadent Croissant French Toast

Two Servings

2 (day-old) croissants

¼ cup cream cheese

8 fresh strawberries

3 eggs

½ cup half-and-half

3 tablespoons sugar

1 teaspoon vanilla extract

Butter, for frying

Confectioners' sugar

Slice croissants lengthwise to make a butterfly shape. Spread 1 tablespoon of the cream cheese on the inside of each croissant half. Slice 4 of the strawberries and place slices on cream cheese. Fold halves together to re-form croissants. In a medium bowl, whisk together eggs, half-and-half, sugar, and vanilla. Soak croissants, dipping both sides in batter but not allowing them to become soggy. In a medium skillet, cook croissants in butter until thoroughly cooked and golden brown on both sides. Garnish with remaining berries. Dust with confectioners' sugar.

Willows Inn
Lummi Island, Washington

Portuguese Peach French Toast

Six Servings

1 can (29 ounces) sliced peaches, drained

¾ cup maple syrup

6 eggs

1 cup half-and-half

Dash ground nutmeg

1 round loaf Hawaiian sweet bread

Confectioners' sugar

In a medium saucepan, bring peaches and maple syrup to a boil. Reduce heat and simmer peaches for 30 minutes. In a medium bowl, beat eggs, half-and-half, and nutmeg. Pour egg mixture into a shallow bowl. Cut bread loaf in half and slice each half into six 1-inch slices. Dip slices of bread into batter, turning to coat both sides.

Heat griddle or skillet over medium heat and grease if necessary. Cook bread on hot griddle until golden brown on both sides. Transfer to platter and sprinkle with confectioners' sugar. Serve with warm peach mixture.

Mayfield House Bed & Breakfast
Tahoe City, California

House Specialties

RISE AND SHINE OATMEAL

MORNING MUESLI MIX

SWISS MUESLI

CRUNCHY NUT GRANOLA

BLUEBERRY RHUBARB CRISP

APPLE OATMEAL CRISP

BLUEBERRY SOURDOUGH COBBLER

FRESH CHERRY COBBLER

RASPBERRY KUCHEN

AUSTRIAN APPLE STRUDEL

"GOOD MORNING" PIE

PEAR DUTCH BABY

APPLE SKILLET PANCAKE

BAKED COTTAGE CHEESE PANCAKE

BREAKFAST BERRY PUDDING

APPLE PIE BREAD PUDDING

BANANA WALNUT BREAD PUDDING

CARAMEL APPLE FRENCH TOAST

PEACHES AND CREAM FRENCH TOAST

CHEESE BLINTZ SOUFFLÉ

EASY STICKY BUNS

ESPRESSO BISCOTTI

MIMOSA TRUFFLES

Rise and Shine Oatmeal

Six Servings

2 cups old-fashioned oats

4 cups milk

¼ teaspoon salt

1 fresh ripe nectarine, peeled and chopped

1 apple, peeled and chopped

1 banana, peeled and chopped

¼ cup raisins

In a large saucepan, combine oats, milk, salt, nectarine, apple, banana, and raisins; let soak for several minutes. Simmer slowly over low heat, stirring frequently. Cook until mixture becomes thickened, about 10 minutes. Serve warm in individual bowls.

Scarlett's Country Inn
Calistoga, California

Morning Muesli Mix

Ten Cups

9 large shredded wheat biscuits, crumbled

3 cups old-fashioned oats

1 cup wheat bran

1 cup wheat germ

¼ cup packed brown sugar

¾ cup raisins, dried cherries, or dried cranberries

¾ cup dried apricots, diced

½ cup sliced almonds

Milk or yogurt (optional)

Fresh fruit (optional)

In a large bowl, combine shredded wheat biscuits, oats, wheat bran, wheat germ, brown sugar, raisins, apricots, and almonds; mix well. Store in an airtight container. Serve with milk or yogurt and fresh fruit, if desired.

The Philo Pottery Inn
Philo, California

Swiss Muesli

Four Servings

1 cup old-fashioned oats

1 cup orange juice

Juice of half a lemon

¼ cup raisins

¼ cup chopped nuts

3 cups chopped fresh fruit, plus more for topping

1 cup plain yogurt

Dash ground cinnamon

Sugar to taste

Whipped cream (optional)

In a large bowl, combine oats, orange juice, and lemon juice. Mix in raisins, nuts, and fruit. Stir in yogurt. Add cinnamon and sugar to taste. Fold in whipped cream, or top with dollops of whipped cream and additional fruit, if desired.

Chalet Luise
Whistler, British Columbia

*House
Specialties*

Crunchy Nut Granola

Eight Cups

6 cups old-fashioned oats

¾ cup broken cashews

¾ cup broken pecans

¾ cup pine nuts

½ cup nut or vegetable oil

½ cup honey

⅓ cup hot water

1½ teaspoons vanilla extract

¾ cup dried fruit (golden raisins, dried cherries, etc.)

Preheat oven to 325°F. In a large bowl, combine oats, cashews, pecans, and pine nuts. In a separate bowl, whisk together oil, honey, water, and vanilla. Add honey mixture to oat mixture; mix well. Transfer mixture to greased jelly roll pan. Bake for about 40 minutes, stirring frequently, until granola is golden brown. Remove from oven; cool. Stir in dried fruit. Store in an airtight container.

Mesa Verde Plantation Bed & Breakfast
Lemon Cove, California

Raspberry Streusel Muffins, page 13
with Fresh Peach Smoothie, page 151

Hazelnut Waffles with Peaches, page 66

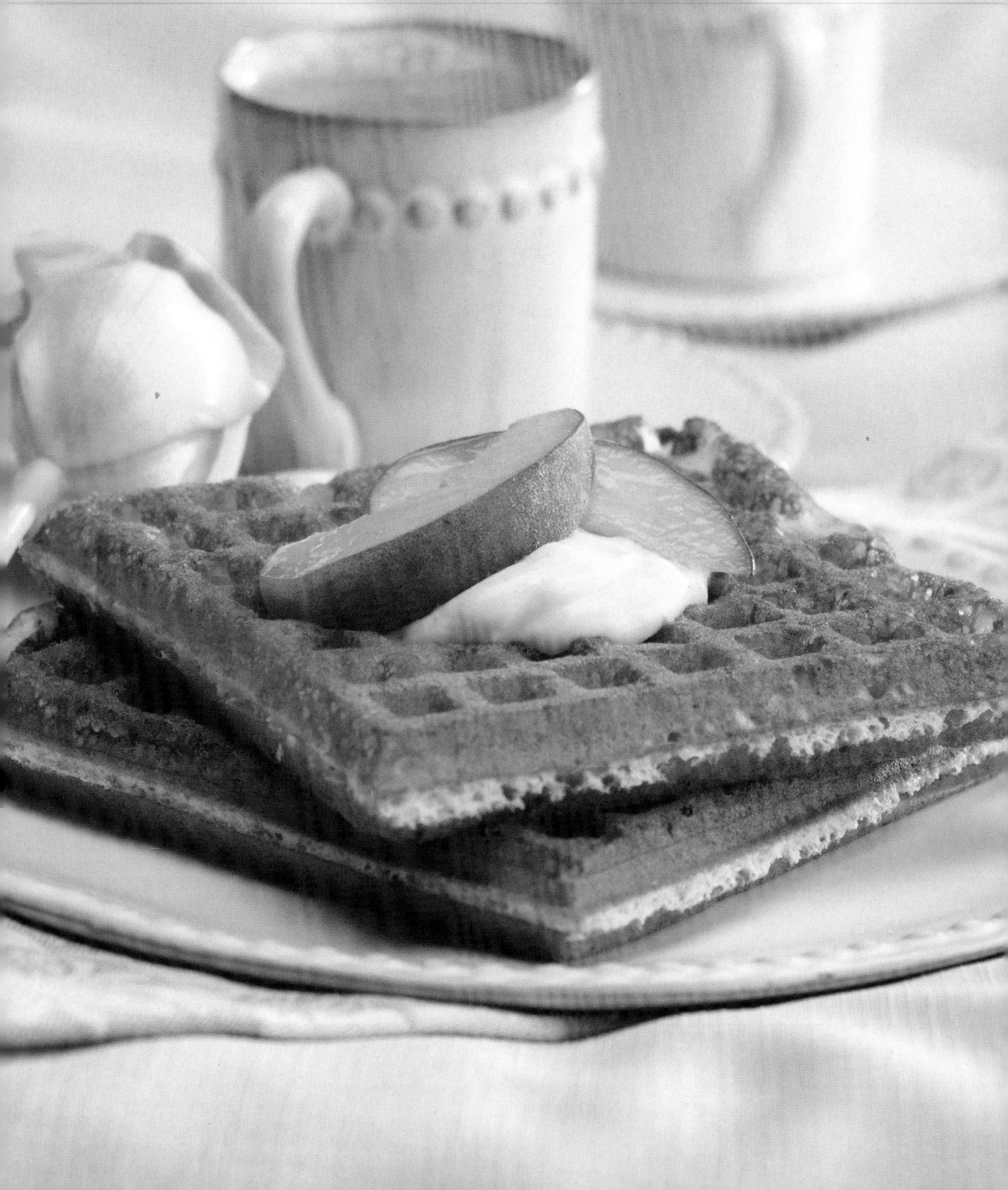

Fresh Fruit Crepes, page 65
with Two Berry Sauce, page 159

Espresso Biscotti, page 104
with Mimosa Truffles, page 105

Creamy Eggs with Caviar, page 110

Eggs Gruyère with Tomato Topping, page 139
with Poached Pears in Raspberry Sauce, page 165

Miniature Ham and Cheese Quiches, page 142

Smoked Salmon Cheesecake, page 141

Blueberry Rhubarb Crisp

Eight Servings

4 cups rhubarb, cut into 1-inch pieces

2 cups blueberries

1 cup granulated sugar

½ cup all-purpose flour

1 teaspoon ground cinnamon

1 teaspoon lemon juice

½ cup water

Topping:

1 cup all-purpose flour

1 cup packed brown sugar

½ cup old-fashioned oats

½ cup (1 stick) butter, melted

½ cup chopped walnuts (optional)

Preheat oven to 375°F. In a large bowl, combine rhubarb, blueberries, sugar, flour, cinnamon, lemon juice, and water; mix well. Pour mixture into a greased 12- by 9-inch baking dish.

For topping, in a small bowl, combine flour, brown sugar, oats, and butter. Add walnuts, if desired. Sprinkle topping over rhubarb mixture. Bake for 45 minutes, or until rhubarb is tender.

Schnauzer Crossing
Bellingham, Washington

Apple Oatmeal Crisp

Six Servings

4 cups peeled and thinly sliced apples

1½ tablespoons fresh lemon juice

3½ tablespoons granulated sugar

Topping:

⅓ cup all-purpose flour

1 cup old-fashioned oats

½ cup packed brown sugar

1 teaspoon ground cinnamon

½ teaspoon salt

½ cup (1 stick) butter, melted

Preheat oven to 375°F. Combine apples, lemon juice, and sugar in a greased 9-inch square baking pan.

For topping, in a medium bowl, combine flour, oats, brown sugar, cinnamon, salt, and butter; spoon evenly over apples. Bake for 35 minutes, or until topping is golden and apples are tender.

Sutter Creek Inn
Sutter Creek, California

Blueberry Sourdough Cobbler

Eight Servings

5 to 6 slices sourdough bread

4 eggs

½ cup milk

¼ teaspoon baking powder

1 teaspoon vanilla extract

½ cup sugar

1½ teaspoons cornstarch

1 teaspoon ground cinnamon

¼ teaspoon ground nutmeg

6 cups fresh or frozen blueberries

3 tablespoons butter, melted

Trim crusts from bread and slice into 1- or 1½-inch fingers. Place on a rimmed cookie sheet. In a medium bowl, beat together eggs, milk, baking powder, and vanilla. Pour over bread until thoroughly covered. Cover with plastic wrap and refrigerate overnight.

Preheat oven to 450°F. In a large bowl, combine sugar, cornstarch, cinnamon, and nutmeg. Stir in blueberries. Spread berries in a greased 13- by 9-inch baking dish. Carefully place bread soaked side up on top of berries, wedging pieces together to make a solid "crust." Drizzle melted butter over top of bread. Bake for 25 minutes, or until crisp and golden brown. Let stand 5 minutes before serving. Cut cobbler into squares and place carefully on plates, spooning juice and berries over top.

Chambered Nautilus
Seattle, Washington

Fresh Cherry Cobbler

Nine Servings

1¼ cups sugar

3 tablespoons cornstarch

4 cups fresh, pitted sweet cherries

¼ teaspoon almond extract

Topping:

1 cup all-purpose flour

1 tablespoon sugar

1½ teaspoons baking powder

½ teaspoon salt

3 tablespoons shortening

½ cup milk

Whipped cream (optional)

Preheat oven to 400°F. Mix sugar and cornstarch in a medium saucepan. Add cherries and almond extract. Cook over medium heat, stirring constantly, until mixture thickens and comes to a boil. Stir for 1 minute. Pour into an ungreased 8-inch square baking pan. Keep fruit mixture hot in oven while preparing biscuit topping.

For topping, in a medium bowl, mix flour, sugar, baking powder, and salt. Cut in shortening until mixture resembles fine crumbs. Stir in milk; mix until dough forms ball. Drop dough by spoonfuls onto hot fruit. Bake for 25 minutes, or until topping is golden brown. Serve warm with whipped cream, if desired.

Rockwood Gardens Bed & Breakfast
Mariposa, California

Raspberry Kuchen

Sixteen Squares

1 egg, well beaten

½ cup sugar

½ cup milk

2 tablespoons vegetable oil

1 cup all-purpose flour

2 teaspoons baking powder

1 cup fresh raspberries

Topping:

½ cup all-purpose flour

½ cup sugar

3 tablespoons butter

Preheat oven to 375°F. In a large bowl, combine egg, sugar, milk, and oil; mix well. In a medium bowl, sift together flour and baking powder; stir into egg mixture. Pour batter into a greased 8-inch square cake pan. Sprinkle raspberries over batter.

For topping, in a small bowl, mix flour and sugar. Cut in butter until mixture resembles coarse crumbs. Sprinkle topping over raspberries. Bake for 25 to 30 minutes, or until a toothpick inserted into center of cake comes out clean.

Belle de Jour Inn
Healdsburg, California

Austrian Apple Strudel

Six Servings

1 sheet frozen prepared puff pastry

2 tablespoons butter

1 large green apple, peeled and chopped into ½-inch pieces

⅓ cup golden raisins

10 dried apricot halves, cut into quarters

⅓ cup chopped walnuts

¼ cup water

¼ cup packed light brown sugar

½ teaspoon ground cinnamon

¼ teaspoon ground nutmeg

1 egg yolk beaten with 1 tablespoon water

Remove puff pastry from freezer and thaw for 20 minutes. In a large skillet, melt butter over medium heat. Add apple, raisins, apricots, and walnuts. Mix well and sauté for a few minutes. Add water, brown sugar, cinnamon, and nutmeg. Cover and simmer for 10 minutes, or until apples are tender but not mushy. Remove from skillet; set aside to cool. Place pastry on a flat surface and distribute apple mixture down center. Make 2-inch cuts diagonally along both sides of pastry at 1-inch intervals. Fold strips over apples, alternating from left to right. Press dough together where ends overlap. Seal top and bottom edges of dough with the tines of a fork. Refrigerate 30 minutes, or freeze for future baking.

Preheat oven to 425°F. Place strudel on a cookie sheet covered with parchment paper. Brush top with egg wash and bake for 25 minutes, or until pastry is puffed and just golden brown.

Chalet de France
Eureka, California

"Good Morning" Pie

Six Servings

2 cups cottage cheese

3 eggs

⅔ cup sugar

2 tablespoons all-purpose flour

1 teaspoon grated orange zest

1 tablespoon orange juice

¼ teaspoon orange extract

9-inch deep-dish pie shell, thawed if frozen

Preheat oven to 350°F. In a large bowl, beat cottage cheese with an electric mixer on high speed for 1 minute. Add eggs, sugar, flour, orange zest, orange juice, and orange extract; blend well. Pour mixture into pie shell and bake for 50 minutes, or until a knife inserted comes out clean. Refrigerate overnight; serve chilled the next morning.

The Blair House Bed & Breakfast Inn
Friday Harbor, Washington

Pear Dutch Baby

Four Servings

2 tablespoons butter

5 eggs

½ cup milk or cream

½ cup all-purpose flour

1 to 2 ripe pears, peeled or unpeeled, sliced

Juice of 1 lemon

Confectioners' sugar

Preheat oven to 450°F. Melt butter in a 9-inch nonstick skillet. Pour half of butter into a medium bowl. Beat eggs into butter. Add milk and flour; mix well. Sauté pears briefly in reserved butter in skillet. Drizzle pears with lemon juice and sprinkle lightly with confectioners' sugar. Arrange pears in pretty pattern in bottom of skillet. Pour egg mixture over pears. (Wrap skillet handle with foil if not ovenproof.) Bake for 20 to 25 minutes, or until top is puffy and golden brown. Invert onto serving platter. Dust with confectioners' sugar. Slice into quarters and serve immediately.

Glenelly Inn
Glen Ellen, California

Apple Skillet Pancake

Two Servings

2 eggs

1 cup milk

3 tablespoons melted butter

¾ cup all-purpose flour

½ teaspoon salt

3 tablespoons sugar, divided

¼ teaspoon ground cinnamon

1½ Golden Delicious apples, peeled and thinly sliced

Preheat oven to 425°F. In a medium bowl, beat eggs, milk, and butter. Stir in flour, salt, and 1 tablespoon of the sugar; mix well. Pour batter into a greased 10-inch cast-iron skillet. Combine 1 tablespoon of the sugar with cinnamon; toss with apple slices. Arrange apple wedges on batter in a pinwheel design. Bake for 20 minutes. Reduce oven temperature to 350°F. Bake for 10 minutes, or until edges are puffed and center is set. Sprinkle with remaining sugar. Slice in half and serve immediately.

The Swedish House Bed & Breakfast
Truckee, California

Baked Cottage Cheese Pancake

Six Servings

½ cup (1 stick) butter

5 eggs

1 tablespoon sugar

1 teaspoon salt (optional)

2 cups milk

1 cup all-purpose flour

1 cup small-curd cottage cheese

1 teaspoon baking powder

Fresh berries and confectioners' sugar (optional)

Preheat oven to 425°F. Cut butter into small pieces and place in a 10-inch cast-iron skillet or a 13- by 9-inch glass baking dish. Heat in oven until butter is melted. Combine eggs, sugar, and salt, if desired, in a blender or electric mixer; mix at high speed for 1 minute. Continue to mix while slowly adding milk, then flour, then cottage cheese, then baking powder. Pour blended mixture into hot skillet or baking dish. Bake for 35 minutes, or until pancake is puffed and beginning to brown. Remove from oven. Let sit 5 to 8 minutes before cutting (center may fall). Serve with fresh berries and confectioners' sugar, if desired.

Frampton House Bed & Breakfast
Healdsburg, California

Breakfast Berry Pudding

Four Servings

4 slices day-old white bread

3 to 4 ounces cream cheese

Cinnamon sugar (1 tablespoon granulated sugar mixed with
¼ teaspoon ground cinnamon)

1 cup fresh raspberries or blueberries

¼ cup packed brown sugar, divided

1 tablespoon butter, diced

4 eggs

1 cup milk

1 teaspoon vanilla extract

Fresh berry sauce and sour cream (optional)

Preheat oven to 350°F. Spread each bread slice with cream cheese and sprinkle with cinnamon sugar. Cube bread and place in bottom of greased 8-inch square baking pan. Distribute raspberries evenly over bread. Sprinkle 2 tablespoons of the brown sugar and butter over cubes. In a medium bowl, beat together eggs, milk, and vanilla; pour over cubes. Sprinkle with remaining brown sugar. Set pan in a larger shallow pan; add 1 inch hot water to shallow pan after pan has been placed on oven rack. Bake for 35 to 40 minutes, or until a toothpick inserted into center of pudding comes out clean. Cool pudding before cutting into squares. Serve in a pool of berry sauce and top with a dollop of sour cream, if desired.

Blue Spruce Inn
Soquel, California

Apple Pie Bread Pudding

Twelve Servings

1 loaf French bread, cut into 1-inch cubes

8 eggs

8 ounces cream cheese

3 cups buttermilk

¼ cup sugar

1 tablespoon vanilla extract

¼ teaspoon salt

1 can (21 ounces) cinnamon and spice apple pie filling

Cinnamon sugar (2 tablespoons sugar mixed with
   ½ teaspoon ground cinnamon)

Distribute bread cubes evenly in a greased 13- by 9-inch baking pan. In a large bowl, beat eggs, cream cheese, buttermilk, sugar, vanilla, and salt. Stir in pie filling; mix well. Pour batter over bread cubes. Sprinkle lightly with cinnamon sugar. Cover and refrigerate overnight.

Preheat oven to 350°F. Uncover pan and bake for 45 to 60 minutes, or until pudding is puffed and golden brown. Let stand 5 minutes before serving.

Murphy's Inn
Grass Valley, California

Banana Walnut Bread Pudding

Ten Servings

1 large loaf banana nut bread, cut into cubes

2 ripe bananas, thinly sliced

12 eggs

2 cups milk

½ cup chopped walnuts

½ teaspoon ground cinnamon

3 tablespoons sugar

Cream Sauce:

1 cup milk

½ cup (1 stick) butter

¼ cup sugar

Preheat oven to 325°F. Toss bread cubes with banana slices; distribute evenly in a greased 13- by 9-inch baking pan. In a large bowl, beat eggs and milk. Pour egg mixture over bread and bananas. In a small bowl, mix walnuts, cinnamon, and sugar; sprinkle over bread mixture. Bake for 1 hour, or until a toothpick inserted into center of pudding comes out clean. Let set 5 to 10 minutes before cutting.

For cream sauce, in a medium saucepan, bring milk, butter, and sugar to a boil. Boil for about 5 minutes, stirring constantly, until froth settles down and sugar is dissolved. Remove from heat; allow to cool slightly. Serve pudding with warm cream sauce.

Anderson Creek Inn
Boonville, California

Caramel Apple French Toast

Six Servings

½ cup (1 stick) butter

1 cup packed brown sugar

2 tablespoons light corn syrup

1 cup chopped pecans

12 slices sweet French bread, ¾ inch thick

6 to 8 green apples, peeled and thinly sliced

6 eggs

1½ cups milk

1 teaspoon vanilla extract

½ teaspoon ground cinnamon

⅛ teaspoon ground nutmeg

Whipped cream (optional)

In a small saucepan, heat butter, brown sugar, and corn syrup over medium heat; stir constantly until thickened. Spray a 13- by 9-inch glass baking dish with nonstick cooking spray. Pour butter mixture into dish; sprinkle with pecans. Arrange 6 bread slices over pecans; top with apple slices. Combine eggs, milk, vanilla, cinnamon, and nutmeg in a blender; process until fully blended. Pour half of egg mixture over apples; top with second layer of bread. Pour remaining egg mixture over bread. Cover and refrigerate overnight.

Preheat oven to 350°F. Bake uncovered for 50 to 60 minutes, or until French toast is golden brown. Serve with whipped cream, if desired.

Whitegate Inn Bed & Breakfast
Mendocino, California

Peaches and Cream French Toast

Six Servings

10 to 12 slices white bread, crusts removed

3 eggs

2 cups half-and-half

½ cup sugar

1 teaspoon vanilla extract

1 can (16 ounces) peach halves, drained and cut horizontally into
    ¼-inch slices

Dash ground nutmeg

Filling:

8 ounces cream cheese

¼ cup sugar

1 egg

1 teaspoon vanilla extract

Arrange half of bread in bottom of a greased 11- by 7-inch glass baking dish. In a medium bowl, beat eggs, half-and-half, sugar, and vanilla. Pour half of egg mixture over bread.

For filling, in a medium bowl, beat cream cheese, sugar, egg, and vanilla; pour evenly over bread mixture. Place peaches over filling. Arrange remaining bread slices over peaches. Pour remaining egg mixture over bread. Sprinkle with nutmeg. Cover and refrigerate overnight.

Preheat oven to 350°F. Cover and bake for 30 minutes. Uncover and bake for 30 to 40 minutes, or until French toast is puffy and golden brown.

Pelican Cove Inn
Carlsbad, California

Cheese Blintz Soufflé

Six Servings

3 tablespoons butter, melted

1 box (13 ounces) frozen cheese blintzes

4 eggs

1¼ cups sour cream

¼ cup orange juice

½ cup sugar

2 teaspoons vanilla extract

Dash salt

Pour butter into an 11- by 7-inch glass baking dish. Place blintzes in dish in a single layer. In a medium bowl, beat eggs, sour cream, orange juice, sugar, vanilla, and salt; pour over frozen blintzes. Cover and refrigerate overnight.

Preheat oven to 350°F. Uncover dish and bake for 45 to 55 minutes, or until soufflé is puffed and golden brown.

Melitta Station Inn
Santa Rosa, California

Easy Sticky Buns

Sixteen Servings

½ cup pecans, divided

½ cup (1 stick) butter

1 cup packed light brown sugar

2 tablespoons water

2 tubes (8 ounces each) crescent dinner rolls

½ cup raisins, divided

1 teaspoon ground cinnamon, divided

Preheat oven to 350°F. Sprinkle ¼ cup of the pecans in the bottom of a greased fluted tube pan. In a small saucepan, combine butter, brown sugar, water, and the remaining pecans. Bring mixture to a boil and simmer for 1 minute. Pour half of the mixture over the pecans in the pan. Slice each roll of crescent dough into 8 pieces. Arrange the contents of one tube of rolls over the brown sugar mixture in the pan. Sprinkle with ¼ cup of the raisins and ½ teaspoon of the cinnamon. Spoon remaining brown sugar mixture over the raisins and cinnamon. Place remaining dough slices on top, overlapping the lower slices. Sprinkle the remaining raisins and cinnamon over the dough. Bake for 25 minutes, or until buns are golden brown. Cool on a rack for 10 minutes, then invert pan to unmold buns.

The Bed & Breakfast Inn
San Francisco, California

Espresso Biscotti

Twenty-Four Biscotti

1 egg

4 teaspoons milk

¼ cup plus 1 tablespoon espresso or strong coffee

1 cup sugar

1 teaspoon vanilla extract

2 cups all-purpose flour

½ teaspoon baking powder

½ teaspoon baking soda

½ teaspoon salt

½ teaspoon ground cinnamon

¼ teaspoon ground cloves

¾ cup mini chocolate chips

¾ cup finely chopped walnuts

¾ cup dried cranberries or cherries

Preheat oven to 350°F. In a large bowl, beat egg, milk, espresso, sugar, and vanilla. Stir in flour, baking powder, baking soda, salt, cinnamon, and cloves; mix well. Fold in chocolate chips, walnuts, and cranberries. Place dough onto greased and floured baking sheet. Pat into a ½-inch-thick rectangle, about 12 by 4 inches. Bake for 20 to 25 minutes, or until a toothpick inserted into center comes out clean. Cool 15 minutes.

Decrease oven temperature to 300°F. Cut log crosswise into ½-inch slices. Place slices cut side down on baking sheet. Bake for 15 minutes, turning once. Cool on a wire rack.

Agate Cove Inn Bed & Breakfast
Mendocino, California

Mimosa Truffles

Forty Truffles

10 ounces bittersweet chocolate

1 cup confectioners' sugar, divided

2 egg yolks

½ cup heavy (whipping) cream

¼ cup (½ stick) butter

1 ounce Grand Marnier

2 ounces champagne

Cocoa powder

Melt chocolate in a double boiler or microwave; set aside. In a medium bowl, beat ½ cup of the confectioners' sugar and egg yolks. In a saucepan or double boiler, bring cream, remaining confectioners' sugar, and butter to a boil, stirring constantly; cool slightly. Whisk cream mixture into yolk mixture. Gradually add melted chocolate, Grand Marnier, and champagne; stir until well blended. Refrigerate 4 hours or until set.

Roll into balls, 1 inch in diameter. Roll balls in cocoa powder. Keep refrigerated.

Inn on Summer Hill
Summerland, California

SCRAMBLED EGGS WITH SMOKED SALMON

CREAMY EGGS WITH CAVIAR

HAWAIIAN SCRAMBLE

DIVINE FILLED CROISSANTS

ANGEL EGGS

POACHED EGGS MADISON

SEASHELL EGG BAKE

BAKED EGGS FLORENTINE

EASY EGGS BENEDICT

HAM AND CHEESE BAKED EGGS

MINI CHEDDAR CHEESE SOUFFLÉS

CRAB SOUFFLÉ

CHEESY CORNMEAL SOUFFLÉ

BAKED EGGS WITH TWO CHEESES

ITALIAN ZUCCHINI PIE

SPINACH MUSHROOM QUICHE

SOUTH OF THE BORDER CRUSTLESS QUICHE

GREEN CHILE AND POTATO PIE

HAM AND CHEESE CRUSTLESS QUICHE

HASH BROWN QUICHE

CHILES RELLENOS BAKE

ARTICHOKE MUSHROOM BAKE

PEPPERONI EGG CASSEROLE

Morning Egg Dishes

Scrambled Eggs with Smoked Salmon

Four Servings

2 tablespoons butter

10 eggs

⅛ teaspoon white pepper

4 ounces smoked salmon, flaked

6 tablespoons half-and-half or milk

4 dashes Worcestershire sauce

4 drops Tabasco sauce

Melt butter in a double boiler. In a large bowl, whisk eggs. Add white pepper, salmon, half-and-half, Worcestershire sauce, and Tabasco sauce. Pour egg mixture into double boiler and stir until thick and creamy. Serve immediately.

Mattey House
McMinnville, Oregon

Creamy Eggs with Caviar

Six Servings

2 tablespoons butter, divided

1 tablespoon all-purpose flour

½ cup sour cream, plus more for garnish

12 eggs

¼ teaspoon salt

Pinch white pepper

6 puff pastry rectangles, baked

Caviar

In a small saucepan, melt 1 tablespoon of the butter over medium heat. Stir in flour; cook until bubbly. Remove from heat and blend in sour cream. Return to heat and cook until bubbly and smooth; set aside. In a large bowl, beat eggs, salt, and white pepper. In a large skillet, melt remaining butter over medium heat. Pour in eggs and cook gently, lifting cooked portion to allow uncooked portion to flow underneath, until eggs are softly set. Remove from heat and gently stir in sour cream mixture. Serve eggs on baked puff pastry rectangles. Top with a dollop of sour cream and a sprinkling of caviar.

North Coast Country Inn
Gualala, California

Hawaiian Scramble

Four Servings

10 eggs

Salt and pepper to taste

1½ cups cooked ham, cubed

¾ cup pineapple tidbits, drained

1½ cups shredded Swiss cheese, divided

Preheat broiler. In a large bowl, beat eggs with salt and pepper. Pour into a lightly greased nonstick skillet. Stir eggs over medium heat until set but still soft. In a separate skillet, warm ham cubes. Add ham to eggs along with pineapple and 1 cup of the cheese; continue to cook until eggs are set. Spoon eggs into 4 au gratin dishes. Sprinkle with remaining cheese and broil just until cheese is melted.

The Old Brick Silo Bed & Breakfast
Leavenworth, Washington

Divine Filled Croissants

Four Servings

4 large croissants

4 tablespoons butter

8 eggs

¼ cup milk

1 tablespoon snipped fresh dill (or 1 teaspoon dried)

½ cup finely chopped mushrooms

⅓ cup finely chopped smoked salmon

½ cup shredded Monterey Jack cheese

Preheat oven to 225°F. Warm croissants in oven for 5 to 10 minutes. Meanwhile, melt butter in a medium skillet. In a large bowl, beat eggs and milk; add dill, mushrooms, and salmon. Pour into skillet and scramble until eggs are creamy and just set.

Preheat broiler. Remove croissants from oven and slice lengthwise about three-fourths of the way through (like a clamshell). Fill the croissants with the scrambled eggs and sprinkle with cheese. Broil croissants open-face, just until cheese is melted. Serve immediately.

Grouse Mountain Bed & Breakfast
North Vancouver, British Columbia

Angel Eggs

Six Servings

2 tablespoons sesame seed oil

2 cups angel hair pasta, cooked and drained

1½ cups diced tomato

1 cup chopped onion

½ cup minced Anaheim green chiles

¼ teaspoon pepper

⅛ teaspoon salt

4 eggs, lightly beaten

½ cup half-and-half

½ cup shredded Monterey Jack cheese

½ cup shredded Gruyère cheese

Sour cream and salsa (optional)

In a large skillet, heat oil. Add the pasta and toss until heated through and slightly brown. Add tomato, onion, chiles, pepper, and salt; toss and sauté for 2 minutes. In a medium bowl, combine eggs and half-and-half. Pour egg mixture over pasta and cook over medium heat for 5 minutes, without stirring. Sprinkle cheese over eggs. Cover pan and reduce heat. Cook for 5 minutes, or until eggs are set. Remove from heat; cut into wedges. Serve immediately with sour cream and salsa, if desired.

Bombay House
Bainbridge Island, Washington

Poached Eggs Madison

Four Servings

2 cups shredded lettuce

2 large avocados

8 eggs

1 cup salsa

1½ cups shredded sharp cheddar cheese

½ cup sour cream

4 black olives, cut in half

4 flour tortillas

Place ½ cup shredded lettuce on each plate. Cut avocados in half; peel and remove pit. Slice each half horizontally to make two flat slices; place on individual plates. Meanwhile, poach eggs and heat salsa. Place 2 poached eggs on top of avocado slices. Spoon warm salsa over eggs. Sprinkle with shredded cheese. Garnish with sour cream and olive halves. Heat tortillas on a hot griddle, 10 seconds on each side. Fold tortillas into fourths. Serve tortillas with eggs.

Madison Street Inn
Santa Clara, California

Seashell Egg Bake

Two Servings

1 slice bacon, fried

1 cup shredded Swiss cheese, divided

2 eggs

2 teaspoons whipping cream

Salt and pepper to taste

Preheat oven to 350°F. Crumble bacon into small pieces; set aside. Spray two 3-inch-long seashells with nonstick cooking spray. Sprinkle cheese on bottom of each shell, enough to cover. Crack an egg onto each bed of cheese. Add cream, salt, and pepper on top of eggs. Sprinkle with bacon pieces and remaining cheese. Bake for 10 minutes, or until eggs are firm. Serve immediately.

Log Castle Bed & Breakfast
Langley, Washington

Baked Eggs Florentine

Four Servings

16 to 20 fresh spinach leaves

1 teaspoon butter

4 tablespoons grated Parmesan cheese

4 large eggs

4 tablespoons whipping cream

Freshly ground pepper

Preheat oven to 375°F. Spray 4 medium ramekins with nonstick cooking spray. Lightly steam spinach leaves in butter until wilted; let cool. Line ramekins with spinach leaves. Place 1 teaspoon of the cheese over each bed of spinach. Gently crack an egg into each ramekin. Pour 1 tablespoon of the cream around each egg. Sprinkle with remaining cheese and a dash of pepper. Bake for 10 to 12 minutes, or until eggs are firm.

Blue House Inn
Langley, Washington

Easy Eggs Benedict

Six Servings

6 slices Canadian bacon or turkey ham

6 slices (1 ounce each) Swiss cheese

12 eggs

¼ cup heavy (whipping) cream

Pepper to taste

Dash paprika

Grated Parmesan cheese

English muffins (optional)

Preheat oven to 450°F. Spray 6 large ramekins or custard cups with nonstick cooking spray. Place 1 slice Canadian bacon in bottom of each ramekin; top with 1 slice Swiss cheese. Gently crack two eggs on top of cheese. Pour 1 tablespoon of the cream into each ramekin. Bake for 8 minutes, or until egg whites are firm (yolks may be soft). Sprinkle with pepper, paprika, and Parmesan cheese. Serve with toasted English muffins, if desired.

Loma Vista Bed & Breakfast
Temecula, California

Ham and Cheese Baked Eggs

Four Servings

4 large ham slices

6 eggs

1 teaspoon Dijon mustard

½ cup plain yogurt

1½ cups shredded cheddar cheese, divided

2 teaspoons snipped fresh chives, divided

2 teaspoons chopped fresh parsley, divided

Fresh herb sprigs (optional)

Preheat oven to 375°F. Place 1 slice ham in 4 greased large ramekins or custard cups. In a medium bowl, beat eggs, mustard, and yogurt. Stir ½ cup of the cheese, 1 teaspoon of the chives, and 1 teaspoon of the parsley into egg mixture; mix well. Spoon egg mixture evenly over ham in ramekins. Sprinkle remaining cheese, chives, and parsley into ramekins. Bake for 25 to 30 minutes, or until cheese is golden and eggs are set. Garnish with fresh herb sprigs, if desired.

The Hanford House Bed & Breakfast Inn
Sutter Creek, California

Mini Cheddar Cheese Soufflés

Four Servings

¼ cup (½ stick) butter

¼ cup all-purpose flour

Dash paprika

Dash cayenne pepper

1 cup milk

1 cup shredded cheddar cheese

4 eggs, separated

Preheat oven to 375°F. In a medium saucepan, melt butter over medium heat. Stir in flour, paprika, and cayenne pepper. Whisk in milk and cook, stirring constantly, until smooth and slightly thickened. Add cheese and stir until melted; remove from heat. In a small bowl, beat egg yolks slightly; stir into cheese mixture. In a separate bowl, beat egg whites until stiff; fold into cheese mixture. Spoon into 4 greased and floured large ramekins or custard cups. Bake for 15 to 20 minutes, or until eggs are puffed and golden brown. Serve immediately.

The Pelennor Bed & Breakfast
Mariposa, California

Crab Soufflé

Four Servings

8 ounces fresh or imitation crab, chopped

1 cup shredded cheddar cheese

1 cup shredded Monterey Jack cheese

6 eggs

1 cup sour cream

1 tablespoon butter, melted

¼ cup all-purpose flour

½ teaspoon baking powder

¼ teaspoon salt

Preheat oven to 375°F. Spray a 1½-quart soufflé dish with nonstick cooking spray. Layer crab and cheeses in bottom of dish. In a blender, combine eggs, sour cream, butter, flour, baking powder, and salt; blend until smooth. Pour egg mixture over crab. Bake for about 1 hour, or until eggs are set.

Forbestown Bed & Breakfast Inn
Lakeport, California

Cheesy Cornmeal Soufflé

Four Servings

3 tablespoons butter

2 tablespoons chopped green onions

¼ cup yellow cornmeal

½ teaspoon dried oregano

1¼ cups milk

¾ cup shredded Monterey Jack cheese

4 eggs, separated

Fresh Tomato Sauce:

¼ cup (½ stick) butter

4 cups chopped fresh tomatoes

½ teaspoon dried basil

½ teaspoon salt

¼ teaspoon pepper

Preheat oven to 350°F. In a medium saucepan, melt butter and sauté green onions. Stir in cornmeal and oregano. Add milk and cheese. Stir over medium heat until cheese is melted and sauce thickens; remove from heat. Stir in egg yolks. In a small bowl, beat egg whites until soft peaks form. Fold egg whites into cornmeal mixture. Pour into a greased 1½-quart soufflé dish; set in a pan of water. Bake for 45 minutes, or until soufflé is puffed and golden brown.

For sauce, in a medium saucepan, melt butter over medium heat. Add tomatoes, basil, salt, and pepper; simmer for 30 minutes. Serve warm tomato sauce with soufflé.

The Heirloom Bed & Breakfast
Ione, California

Baked Eggs with Two Cheeses

Eight Servings

12 eggs

1 cup milk

Dash salt

Drop of Tabasco

2 cups shredded cheddar cheese

2 cups shredded Monterey Jack cheese or mozzarella cheese

Preheat oven to 325°F. In a blender or large bowl, beat eggs, milk, salt, Tabasco, and cheeses. Pour mixture into an ungreased 8-inch round soufflé dish. Bake for approximately 1 hour, or until eggs are set.

Whispering Pines
Spokane, Washington

Italian Zucchini Pie

Six Servings

1 small onion, chopped

1 clove garlic, minced

1 medium zucchini, sliced

2 large Swiss chard leaves, chopped

2 tablespoons olive oil

6 eggs

1 teaspoon dried basil

1 teaspoon dried oregano

Salt and pepper, to taste

1 cup grated Parmesan cheese

Preheat oven to 350°F. In a medium skillet, sauté onion, garlic, zucchini, and Swiss chard in oil for 5 to 8 minutes, or until vegetables are tender. Remove vegetables from heat; cool slightly. In a medium bowl, beat eggs with basil, oregano, salt, and pepper; stir in cheese. Spoon vegetables into a greased 9-inch pie plate. Pour egg mixture over vegetables. Bake for 25 to 30 minutes, or until pie is puffed and golden brown.

Rancho San Gregorio
San Gregorio, California

Spinach Mushroom Quiche

Six Servings

One 9-inch pie shell, unbaked

½ teaspoon yellow mustard

2 teaspoons butter

½ cup chopped onion

½ cup sliced mushrooms

1 package frozen chopped spinach, thawed and drained

1 cup shredded Swiss cheese

3 eggs

1 cup milk

½ teaspoon salt

Dash paprika

Preheat oven to 400°F. Bake pie shell according to package directions. Reduce oven temperature to 350°F. Spread mustard in bottom of baked pie shell. In a medium skillet, melt butter over medium heat. Sauté onion, mushrooms, and spinach; spoon into pie shell. Sprinkle with cheese. In a medium bowl, beat eggs, milk, and salt; pour over vegetables and cheese. Sprinkle with paprika. Bake for 40 to 45 minutes, or until center is set.

Todd Farm House Bed & Breakfast
Fort Bragg, California

South of the Border Crustless Quiche

Six Servings

6 eggs

2 tablespoons all-purpose flour

2 cups cottage cheese

1 cup shredded Monterey Jack cheese

¼ cup (½ stick) butter, melted

1 can (4 ounces) chopped green chiles, drained

Salsa and sour cream (optional)

Preheat oven to 375°F. In a large bowl, beat eggs. Add flour. Mix in cheeses, butter, and chiles. Pour into a greased 10-inch pie plate. Bake for 30 minutes, or until center is set. Serve with salsa and sour cream, if desired.

Salisbury House
Seattle, Washington

Green Chile and Potato Pie

Six Servings

4 to 5 new red potatoes (unpeeled)

1 large onion, chopped

4 garlic cloves, minced

2 tablespoons olive oil

1 can (4 ounces) chopped green chiles, drained

1 jar (7¼ ounces) roasted red bell peppers, chopped

5 eggs

1 cup shredded Monterey Jack cheese

1 cup shredded medium cheddar cheese

Pinch crushed red pepper

¼ teaspoon salt

Dash black pepper

Preheat oven to 375°F. Wash and boil potatoes until nearly cooked (potatoes should remain firm); set aside. When cool, cut into ¼-inch slices. In a medium skillet, sauté onion and garlic in oil until soft; remove from heat. Add chiles and bell peppers to onion mixture. In a large bowl, beat eggs; stir in onion mixture, cheeses, red pepper, salt, and black pepper. Layer half of the potatoes in a greased 10-inch deep-dish pie plate. Spoon half of egg mixture over potatoes. Repeat with second layer of potatoes and remaining egg mixture. Bake for 30 to 35 minutes, or until pie is golden brown and center is set.

The Stanford Inn by the Sea
Mendocino, California

Ham and Cheese Crustless Quiche

Six Servings

1 can (4 ounces) chopped green chiles, drained

¼ small Spanish onion, finely chopped

1 small tomato, chopped

½ cup shredded Monterey Jack cheese

½ cup shredded cheddar cheese

¾ cup diced ham

4 eggs

½ cup milk

¼ teaspoon dried basil

¼ teaspoon dried oregano

Salt and pepper, to taste

Preheat oven to 375°F. Spray a 9-inch pie plate with nonstick cooking spray. Layer pie plate with chiles, onion, tomato, cheeses, and ham. In a blender, combine eggs, milk, basil, oregano, salt, and pepper; blend until smooth. Pour egg mixture into pie plate. Bake for 30 to 35 minutes, or until center is set.

Barretta Gardens Bed & Breakfast Inn
Sonora, California

Hash Brown Quiche

Six Servings

1 package (24 ounces) frozen shredded hash brown potatoes, thawed

⅓ cup butter, melted

¼ cup ricotta cheese

1 cup shredded cheddar cheese

1 cup shredded Monterey Jack cheese

1 cup diced ham

2 eggs

½ cup milk

⅛ teaspoon cayenne pepper

¼ teaspoon seasoning salt

Preheat oven to 425°F. Press hash brown potatoes into a greased 9-inch pie plate. Brush with butter. Bake for 25 minutes. Reduce oven temperature to 350°F. Spread potatoes with ricotta cheese, then sprinkle with cheddar, Monterey Jack, and ham. In a medium bowl, beat eggs, milk, cayenne pepper, and seasoning salt. Pour egg mixture over cheeses and ham. Bake for 30 to 40 minutes, or until center is set.

Lavender Hill Bed & Breakfast
Sonora, California

Chiles Rellenos Bake

Four Servings

2 cans (4 ounces each) whole green chiles, drained

1½ cups shredded Monterey Jack cheese

3 eggs

1 cup sour cream

Salsa

Preheat oven to 350°F. Arrange chiles in bottom of a greased 9-inch square glass baking dish. Sprinkle cheese over chiles. In a medium bowl, beat eggs and sour cream; pour over chiles and cheese. Bake for about 25 minutes, or until custard is firm in center. Serve warm with salsa.

Flume's End
Nevada City, California

Artichoke Mushroom Bake

Four Servings

3 to 4 tablespoons bread crumbs

1⅔ cups shredded Monterey Jack or cheddar cheese

½ cup chopped onion

½ cup chopped shiitake mushrooms

1 can (14 ounces) artichoke hearts, drained and chopped

3 eggs

⅔ cup milk

½ cup mayonnaise

1 tablespoon cornstarch

BREAKFAST
IN BED

Preheat oven to 350°F. Spray an 8-inch square glass baking dish with nonstick cooking spray. Sprinkle dish generously with bread crumbs. Layer cheese, onion, mushrooms, and artichokes in baking dish. In a medium bowl, beat eggs, milk, mayonnaise, and cornstarch; pour over cheese and vegetables. Bake for 35 to 45 minutes, or until center is set. Let sit 10 minutes before cutting.

Ferrando's Hideaway
Point Reyes Station, California

Pepperoni Egg Casserole

Six Servings

2 cups unseasoned bread cubes

1 cup shredded Monterey Jack cheese

5 eggs

2 cups milk

1 teaspoon Italian seasoning

⅓ cup chopped pepperoni

Preheat oven to 325°F. Place bread cubes in bottom of a greased 10- by 6-inch baking dish. Cover with cheese. In a large bowl, beat eggs, milk, and seasoning; pour over bread and cheese. Top with pepperoni. Bake for 35 to 45 minutes, or until center is set.

Healdsburg Inn on the Plaza
Healdsburg, California

BAKED EGGS FOR A GANG

CHILE CHEESE BAKE

ARTICHOKE MUSHROOM STRATA

GARDEN MEDLEY QUICHE

EGGS GRUYÈRE WITH TOMATO TOPPING

CHEESY SPINACH DELIGHT

SMOKED SALMON CHEESECAKE

MINIATURE HAM AND CHEESE QUICHES

SAUSAGE STRATA

HASH BROWN CASSEROLE

SUNDAY MORNING CASSEROLE

ITALIAN SAUSAGE FRITTATA

BACON AND CHEESE OVEN OMELET

Eggs for a Crowd

Baked Eggs for a Gang

Ten Servings

12 eggs, beaten

2 cans (15 ounces each) creamed corn

1 can (7 ounces) chopped green chiles, drained

1 teaspoon Worcestershire sauce

4 cups shredded sharp cheddar cheese

1 teaspoon salt

½ teaspoon pepper

Preheat oven to 325°F. In a large bowl, combine eggs, corn, chiles, Worcestershire sauce, cheese, salt, and pepper; mix well. Pour into a greased 13- by 9-inch glass baking dish. Bake for 50 to 60 minutes, or until center is set.

Fairview Manor
Ben Lomond, California

Chile Cheese Bake

Ten Servings

6 slices white bread, buttered and crusts trimmed

2 cups shredded sharp cheddar cheese

2 cups shredded Monterey Jack cheese

1 can (4 ounces) chopped green chiles, drained

6 eggs

2 cups milk

2 teaspoons paprika

1 teaspoon salt

½ teaspoon pepper

½ teaspoon dried oregano

¼ teaspoon garlic powder

¼ teaspoon dry mustard

Place bread, buttered side down, in a greased 13- by 9-inch baking dish. Combine cheeses and sprinkle on top of bread. Sprinkle chiles on top of cheese. In a large bowl, beat eggs with milk, paprika, salt, pepper, oregano, garlic powder, and mustard; pour over chiles and let soak into bread. Cover and refrigerate at least 4 hours.

Preheat oven to 325°F. Bake for 55 minutes, or until eggs are golden brown.

Margie's Bed & Breakfast
Sequim, Washington

Artichoke Mushroom Strata

Eight Servings

8 eggs

2 cups milk

2 tablespoons butter, melted

10 slices white bread, crusts removed and cut into ½-inch cubes

1 can (14 ounces) artichoke bottoms, drained and chopped

1 cup shredded Swiss or Muenster cheese

1 cup diced fresh mushrooms

2 tablespoons snipped fresh chives

2 teaspoons dried tarragon

¼ teaspoon salt

¼ teaspoon white pepper

Preheat oven to 375°F. In a blender or large bowl, beat eggs, milk, and butter. In a separate bowl, combine egg mixture with bread, artichokes, cheese, mushrooms, chives, tarragon, salt, and white pepper; let sit 30 minutes. Pour mixture into a 13- by 9-inch greased baking dish. Bake for about 45 minutes, or until strata is puffy and golden brown. (*Note:* This strata can also be baked in 8 large ramekins or custard cups for 30 minutes.)

Old Monterey Inn
Monterey, California

Garden Medley Quiche

Twelve Servings

10 eggs

½ cup all-purpose flour

1 teaspoon baking powder

2 teaspoons onion powder

¼ cup (½ stick) butter, melted

3 cups cottage cheese, divided

1 package (10 ounces) frozen chopped spinach, thawed and squeezed dry

½ red bell pepper, chopped

½ yellow or green bell pepper, chopped

1 bunch green onions, chopped

12 ounces shredded Swiss or Monterey Jack cheese

Preheat oven to 350°F. In a blender or food processor, combine eggs, flour, baking powder, onion powder, butter, and 1 cup of the cottage cheese; blend well. Pour blended mixture into a large bowl and add remaining cottage cheese, spinach, peppers, green onions, and cheese. Mix all ingredients thoroughly. Divide mixture between two greased 10-inch pie pans. Bake for 40 to 45 minutes, or until eggs are set.

Beazley House
Napa, California

Eggs Gruyère with Tomato Topping

Eight Servings

2 cups shredded Gruyère cheese

¼ cup (½ stick) butter, cut into small pieces

1 cup heavy (whipping) cream

1½ teaspoons dry mustard

½ teaspoon salt

⅛ teaspoon white pepper

12 eggs, lightly beaten

Topping:

2 medium tomatoes, cut into ½-inch slices

¼ cup (½ stick) butter

⅔ cup seasoned bread crumbs

⅓ cup unsalted sunflower seeds

Parsley sprigs (optional)

Preheat oven to 325°F. Spray a 13- by 9-inch glass baking dish with nonstick cooking spray. Sprinkle cheese evenly in bottom of dish; dot with butter. In a small bowl, mix cream with mustard, salt, and white pepper; drizzle half of mixture over cheese. Slowly pour eggs over cheese; drizzle with remaining cream mixture. Bake for about 35 minutes, or until eggs are just set.

For topping, during last 20 minutes of baking, place tomato slices on a foil-lined baking sheet and set in oven on bottom shelf. In a small saucepan, melt butter; stir in bread crumbs and sunflower seeds. After 10 minutes, remove tomatoes from oven and top with crumb mixture. Return to oven until eggs are set. Top each serving with a tomato slice and garnish with a parsley sprig, if desired.

The Headlands Inn
Mendocino, California

Cheesy Spinach Delight

Twelve Servings

1½ cups biscuit mix

½ cup milk

5 eggs

1 small onion, chopped

½ cup grated Parmesan cheese

1¼ cups shredded cheddar cheese

2 cups cottage cheese

2 teaspoons minced garlic

1 cup cooked spinach, drained well and patted dry

¾ cup shredded cheddar cheese, for topping

In a medium bowl, combine biscuit mix, milk, and 2 of the eggs. Add onion. Spread mixture in bottom of a greased 13- by 9-inch baking dish. In a separate bowl, mix together remaining eggs, cheeses, garlic, and spinach. Carefully spoon over first layer. Cover and refrigerate overnight.

Preheat oven to 350°F. Uncover dish and bake for 30 minutes, or until center is set. Remove from oven. Let stand 5 minutes before cutting. Sprinkle each serving with 1 tablespoon of the cheese.

Franklin House Bed & Breakfast Inn
Astoria, Oregon

Smoked Salmon Cheesecake

Fourteen Servings

1½ tablespoons butter

½ cup bread crumbs, toasted

¼ cup shredded Gruyère cheese

1 teaspoon chopped fresh dill, or ¼ teaspoon dried

Filling:

1 onion, finely chopped

3 tablespoons butter

1 package (28 ounces) cream cheese, at room temperature

4 eggs

⅓ cup half-and-half

½ cup shredded Gruyère cheese

8 ounces smoked salmon, flaked

Salt to taste

Preheat oven to 325°F. Spread butter on bottom and sides of a 9-inch springform pan. In a small bowl, mix bread crumbs, cheese, and dill together, and sprinkle mixture in pan, turning to coat. Refrigerate.

For filling, in a small skillet, sauté onion in butter. In a large bowl, using a mixer, beat cream cheese and eggs until fluffy. Beat in half-and-half. Fold in cheese, onion, and salmon. Add salt to taste. Pour into prepared pan. Set springform pan in a large roasting pan and add hot water halfway up the sides of the springform pan. Bake for 1 hour and 20 minutes, or until eggs are set. Turn oven off and let cheesecake cool in oven with door ajar for 1 hour. Transfer pan to cooling rack. Let cool to room temperature before serving.

White Swan Inn
San Francisco, California

Miniature Ham and Cheese Quiches

Twelve Miniature Quiches

½ cup (1 stick) butter, softened

3 ounces cream cheese, softened

1 cup all-purpose flour

Filling:

1 can (2¼ ounces) deviled ham

1 small onion, chopped

1 teaspoon butter

½ cup shredded Swiss cheese, divided

1 egg, slightly beaten

¼ cup milk

½ teaspoon ground nutmeg

Dash pepper

In a medium bowl, combine butter and cream cheese; beat until fluffy. Gradually add flour, mixing until smooth. Chill thoroughly.

Preheat oven to 450°F. Divide and shape dough into twelve 1-inch balls. Press dough evenly into 12 miniature muffin cups (2¼ inches in diameter).

For filling, spoon some deviled ham into each cup. In a small skillet, lightly sauté onion in butter; add ¼ cup of the cheese. Mix cheese and onion just to combine and sprinkle mixture over ham. In a small bowl, combine the remaining cheese, egg, milk, nutmeg, and pepper. Spoon mixture evenly into cups. Bake for 10 minutes, then reduce heat to 350°F and bake for 15 minutes, or until custard is set. Serve warm. (*Note:* Cooled quiches can easily be frozen. To reheat, bake at 350°F for 15 minutes.)

The Pringle House Bed & Breakfast
Oakland, Oregon

Sausage Strata

Twelve Servings

1 package (12 ounces) breakfast roll sausage

1 cup finely chopped onion

16 slices sourdough French bread, cut into ½ inch cubes

2 cups shredded sharp cheddar cheese

¼ cup (½ stick) butter, melted

8 eggs

2½ cups milk

In a large skillet, lightly brown sausage, breaking up into small pieces. Add onion; cook until golden brown. Drain off excess fat. In a large bowl, toss bread cubes, cheese, and butter with onion and sausage mixture. Spray a 13- by 9-inch baking pan with nonstick cooking spray. Spread mixture evenly into pan. In a separate bowl, beat eggs and milk together; pour over sausage mixture. Cover with aluminum foil that has been sprayed with nonstick cooking spray. Refrigerate overnight.

Remove pan from refrigerator 30 minutes before baking. Preheat oven to 350°F. Set pan in hot water bath (water should come up the sides of the casserole about ¾ inch). Bake covered for 50 minutes. Uncover and bake for 15 minutes, or until strata is golden brown. Cool 15 minutes before cutting.

The Grey Whale Inn
Fort Bragg, California

Hash Brown Casserole

Eight Servings

1 package (24 ounces) frozen shredded hash brown potatoes, thawed

¼ cup (½ stick) butter, melted

10 slices bacon, cooked crisp

½ cup chopped sun-dried tomatoes

¼ cup chopped fresh parsley

2 cups shredded cheddar cheese

8 eggs

1½ cups milk

½ teaspoon pepper

Crushed tomatoes or salsa (optional)

Preheat oven to 450°F. Press potatoes along bottom and sides of a greased 13- by 9-inch baking pan. Brush potatoes with butter. Bake for 25 minutes. Remove pan from oven. Reduce oven temperature to 350°F. Crumble bacon over potatoes. Sprinkle tomatoes, parsley, and cheese over bacon. In a large bowl, beat eggs, milk, and pepper. Pour egg mixture over cheese. Bake for 45 minutes, or until eggs are set. Let rest 10 minutes before cutting. Serve with crushed tomatoes or salsa, if desired.

The Shore House at Lake Tahoe
Tahoe Vista, California

Sunday Morning Casserole

Eight Servings

16 slices white bread, crusts trimmed

16 slices Canadian bacon or ham

16 slices sharp cheddar cheese

6 eggs

½ teaspoon salt

½ teaspoon pepper

½ teaspoon dry mustard

¼ cup minced onion

¼ cup finely chopped green bell pepper

1 to 2 teaspoons Worcestershire sauce

3 cups milk

Dash Tabasco sauce

Topping:

½ cup (1 stick) butter

¾ cup crushed cornflakes

Place 8 slices of bread in one layer in a greased 13- by 9-inch glass baking dish. Top bread with bacon and then layer cheese. Place remaining bread slices over cheese. In a large bowl, beat eggs with salt, pepper, and mustard. Add onion, bell pepper, Worcestershire sauce, milk, and Tabasco sauce; pour over bread. Cover and refrigerate overnight.

Preheat oven to 350°F. For topping, melt butter and pour over casserole. Top with cornflakes. Bake, uncovered, for 1 hour, or until casserole is golden brown. Remove from oven and let stand 10 minutes before serving.

Pensione Nichols
Seattle, Washington

Italian Sausage Frittata

Eight Servings

1½ pounds mild Italian bulk sausage

3 cups sliced fresh mushrooms

1 teaspoon garlic powder

2 tablespoons butter

¼ cup white wine

3 large Swiss chard leaves, thinly sliced

1 cup shredded cheddar cheese

9 eggs

1¼ cups milk

2 to 3 tablespoons Dijon mustard

Sour cream, salsa, and snipped fresh chives (optional)

Preheat oven to 350°F. In a large skillet, brown sausage; drain. Spread sausage evenly in a greased 13- by 9-inch glass baking dish. Sauté mushrooms and garlic powder in butter and wine until almost all liquid is absorbed; spoon over sausage. Top with Swiss chard and cheese. In a large bowl, beat eggs, milk, and mustard; pour evenly over mushrooms and sausage. Bake for 1 hour or until center is firm to the touch. Cover loosely with foil and let stand 15 minutes before cutting. Serve with sour cream, salsa, and chives, if desired.

La Chaumière, A Country Inn
Calistoga, California

Bacon and Cheese Oven Omelet

Twelve Servings

½ loaf French bread, cut into ½-inch slices

1 cup shredded Gruyère cheese

1 cup shredded Monterey Jack cheese

12 slices bacon, cooked and crumbled

4 green onions, chopped

8 eggs

1⅓ cups milk

⅓ cup white wine

1 teaspoon Dijon mustard

¼ teaspoon black pepper

⅛ teaspoon cayenne pepper

¾ cup sour cream

½ cup grated Parmesan cheese

Dash paprika

Preheat oven to 325°F. Spray a 13-by-9-inch baking dish with nonstick cooking spray. Cover bottom of dish with bread slices. Sprinkle cheeses, bacon, and green onions over bread. In a large bowl, beat eggs, milk, wine, mustard, black pepper, and cayenne pepper; pour over cheese and bread. Cover tightly with foil and bake for 45 minutes, or until center is set. Remove foil and spread with sour cream; sprinkle with Parmesan cheese and paprika. Bake uncovered for about 10 minutes, or until cheese is golden brown. (*Note:* This can be made the night before and refrigerated; let stand at room temperature 30 minutes before baking.)

Strawberry Creek Inn
Idyllwild, California

FRESH PEACH SMOOTHIE

DELICIOUS DATE SHAKE

APPLE CIDER SYRUP

BLACKBERRY SYRUP

HUCKLEBERRY RHUBARB JAM

HAZELNUT HONEY BUTTER

LEMON CURD

GALA ORANGE SAUCE

TWO BERRY SAUCE

ORANGE GINGER SAUCE

BROWN SUGAR SUNSHINE

PEARS EXTRAORDINAIRE

BAKED BANANA CRUMBLE

BROILED SOUR CREAM BLACKBERRIES

POACHED PEARS IN RASPBERRY SAUCE

BAKED BREAKFAST APPLES

SAUSAGE WITH GRAPES

ZESTY SALSA

BREAKFAST POLENTA

BAKED POTATO LATKES

GERMAN POTATO PANCAKES

ROSEMARY ROASTED POTATOES

HOME-FRIED POTATOES AND PEPPERS

Sauces & Side Dishes

Fresh Peach Smoothie

Six Servings

8 large ripe peaches, peeled and chopped

Juice of 2 large oranges

½ cup honey

½ cup crème fraîche or sour cream

Kiwi slices or mint sprigs (optional)

In a blender or food processor, purée the peaches until smooth; add orange juice and mix thoroughly. Add honey and blend completely. Add crème fraîche and mix until smoothie is well blended. Pour into juices glasses. Garnish with kiwi slices, if desired. Serve immediately.

Palmer House Bed & Breakfast Inn
Lincoln City, Oregon

Delicious Date Shake

Four Servings

⅓ cup pitted whole dates

½ cup orange juice

1 pint vanilla ice cream

½ cup plain yogurt

1 teaspoon instant coffee crystals (optional)

In a blender or food processor, combine dates and orange juice; blend until smooth. Add ice cream, yogurt, and coffee crystals, if desired, and process until shake is well blended. Pour into chilled champagne glasses. Serve immediately.

Willcox House Bed & Breakfast
Camano Island, Washington

Apple Cider Syrup

Two Cups

1 cup sugar

2 tablespoons cornstarch

½ teaspoon pumpkin pie spice

2 cups apple cider

2 teaspoons lemon juice

¼ cup (½ stick) butter

In a large saucepan, mix sugar, cornstarch, and pumpkin pie spice. Add apple cider, lemon juice, and butter. Cook over medium heat, stirring frequently, until syrup is thick. Serve warm over pancakes or waffles.

Hilltop Bed & Breakfast
Ferndale, Washington

Blackberry Syrup

Two Cups

2 cups fresh blackberries

¼ cup sugar

½ cup orange juice

In a small saucepan, combine blackberries, sugar, and orange juice. Cook over medium heat for 5 minutes. Lower heat when sauce begins to simmer; continue cooking for about 15 minutes. Serve warm over pancakes, waffles, or ice cream.

Moon & Sixpence
Friday Harbor, Washington

Huckleberry Rhubarb Jam

Four and One-Half Cups

1½ cups crushed huckleberries

¾ cup cooked, mashed rhubarb

3½ cups sugar

One 3-ounce pouch liquid pectin

In a large Dutch oven, combine huckleberries, rhubarb, and sugar; mix well. Place over high heat and bring to a full boil. Boil for 1 minute, stirring constantly. Remove from heat and stir in pectin. Alternately stir and skim for 5 minutes; discard floating fruit. Ladle into hot, sterilized jars and seal.

Marianna Stoltz House Bed & Breakfast
Spokane, Washington

Hazelnut Honey Butter

One and One-Half Cups

¼ cup (½ stick) butter, softened

1 cup honey, at room temperature

1 teaspoon vanilla extract

¼ cup chopped hazelnuts

With an electric mixer or food processor, whip butter, honey, and vanilla; add hazelnuts. (*Note:* Hazelnuts can be chopped quickly in a blender.) Store butter covered in refrigerator. Serve with pancakes, waffles, or muffins.

McGillivray's Log Home Bed & Breakfast
Elmira, Oregon

Lemon Curd

One Cup

4 pasturized egg yolks plus 1 pasturized egg white

¼ cup (½ stick) butter

¾ cup sugar

Juice and grated zest of 1 lemon

In a small bowl, beat together egg yolks and egg white. In a double boiler, melt butter. Stir in sugar, lemon juice, and lemon zest. Add eggs; mix well. Cook slowly over medium-low heat, stirring constantly, for 15 minutes, or until curd is thickened. Cool before covering. Refrigerate up to 2 weeks. Serve with scones, muffins, or toast.

Simpson House Inn
Santa Barbara, California

Gala Orange Sauce

Two Cups

1 cup (2 sticks) butter

1 cup sugar

⅔ cup frozen orange juice concentrate

In a medium saucepan, melt butter over medium heat. Add sugar and orange juice concentrate; stir until sugar is dissolved. Remove from heat and cool slightly. Whip with whisk until sauce is thick and shiny. Serve warm over French toast, waffles, or bread pudding.

Butterfield Bed & Breakfast
Julian, California

Two Berry Sauce

Two Cups

2 cups fresh or frozen raspberries

2 cups fresh or frozen strawberries

⅓ cup sugar

⅓ cup freshly squeezed orange juice

3 tablespoons lemon juice

In a medium saucepan, heat berries, sugar, orange juice, and lemon juice over medium heat. Cook, stirring constantly, until fruit begins to break up, about 5 minutes. Purée in a food processor or blender. Return sauce to saucepan; heat until warm. Serve with waffles, pancakes, or crepes.

Hope-Merrill House
Geyserville, California

Orange Ginger Sauce

One and One-Half Cups

2 tablespoons peeled, minced fresh ginger

½ teaspoon grated orange zest

½ cup orange juice

½ cup water

2 tablespoons light corn syrup

1 cup sugar

In a small saucepan, combine ginger, orange zest, orange juice, water, corn syrup, and sugar; bring to a boil. Boil for 5 minutes over medium-high heat. Serve over pancakes, waffles, or French toast.

The Lookout Bed & Breakfast
Nanoose Bay, British Columbia

Brown Sugar Sunshine

Two Servings

1 medium grapefruit

2 generous tablespoons port wine

2 tablespoons light brown sugar

2 tablespoons butter, melted

Preheat broiler. Cut grapefruit in half. Run a knife along the inner contours of the rind to remove the flesh in one piece. Reserve rind, and place skinned grapefruit mounds upside down on cutting surface; cut each like a pie into 6 sections. Replace grapefruit in shell and place in a baking dish. Spoon 1 tablespoon port on each half. Cover surface with 1 tablespoon brown sugar on each half. Drizzle with butter. Let stand a few minutes (the longer the better). Broil for 10 minutes, or until grapefruit is bubbly and golden brown. Place each half in a small bowl and top with remaining liquid from baking dish.

F. W. Hastings House–Old Consulate Inn
Port Townsend, Washington

Pears Extraordinaire

Four Servings

⅓ cup cream cheese, softened

1 tablespoon honey

1 teaspoon vanilla extract

2 firm fresh pears, peeled

2 tablespoons water

In a small bowl, combine cream cheese, honey, and vanilla; set aside. Cut pears in half lengthwise and remove cores. Place cut side down in a microwave-safe baking dish. Add water. Poach in microwave at full power for 2 to 3 minutes, or until pears are soft. Spoon one-fourth of the cream cheese mixture into each pear half. Serve immediately.

Home by the Sea
Clinton, Washington

Baked Banana Crumble

Four Servings

4 ripe firm bananas, peeled

¾ cup orange juice

1 teaspoon vanilla extract

½ cup all-purpose flour

½ cup quick-cooking oats

¾ cup packed brown sugar

½ teaspoon ground nutmeg

½ teaspoon salt

6 tablespoons cold butter

Vanilla yogurt or ice cream (optional)

Preheat oven to 375°F. Slice bananas lengthwise and place, cut side up, in 4 greased oval ramekins or custard cups. In a small bowl, combine orange juice and vanilla; drizzle over bananas. In a large bowl, combine flour, oats, brown sugar, nutmeg, and salt. Cut in butter until mixture resembles small peas. Spoon crumble mixture evenly over fruit. Bake for 15 to 20 minutes. Serve warm with vanilla yogurt, if desired.

Elk Cove Inn
Elk, California

Broiled Sour Cream Blackberries

Six Servings

3 cups fresh blackberries

1 cup sour cream

1 teaspoon vanilla extract

1 cup packed brown sugar

Preheat broiler. Divide blackberries evenly among 6 small ramekins or custard cups. In a small bowl, mix sour cream and vanilla; spoon over berries. Sprinkle liberally with brown sugar. Broil for 1 minute, or until sugar caramelizes (watch very carefully). Cover and refrigerate several hours or overnight. (*Note:* This recipe can also be made with blueberries or sliced strawberries.)

Tiffany House Bed & Breakfast
Redding, California

Poached Pears in Raspberry Sauce

Four Servings

4 Bosc pears, peeled

¼ cup maple syrup

Cinnamon sugar (1 tablespoon granulated sugar mixed with
 ¼ teaspoon ground cinnamon)

4 teaspoons brown sugar

Whole fresh raspberries (optional)

Sauce:

3 cups fresh or frozen (thawed) raspberries

Granulated sugar

Cut thin slice off bottom of pears so they will stand upright. Place pears in a microwave-safe dish. Spoon 1 tablespoon of the maple syrup over each pear. Sprinkle pears with cinnamon sugar. Sprinkle each pear with 1 teaspoon brown sugar. Cover dish completely with plastic wrap; microwave on high for 10 to 12 minutes, or until pears are tender but not too soft.

For the sauce, place berries in a blender; blend until smooth. Strain sauce through sieve. Add sugar to taste. Place sauce in a medium saucepan and heat until warm. Place each poached pear on a plate and cover with sauce, or spoon sauce on plate and set pear in center. Garnish with raspberries, if desired.

Abigail's "Elegant Victorian Mansion" Bed & Breakfast
Eureka, California

Baked Breakfast Apples

Four Servings

4 large tart apples, unpeeled

¼ cup packed brown sugar

1 teaspoon ground cinnamon

2 tablespoons dried currants

Zest of ½ orange

4 teaspoons butter, cut up

¾ cup apple juice

Whipped cream (optional)

Preheat oven to 375°F. Wash apples and remove core, leaving a ½ inch at bottom. In a small bowl, mix brown sugar, cinnamon, currants, and orange zest. Fill apple centers with brown sugar mixture and dot with butter. Place apples in an 8-inch square baking pan. Pour apple juice in pan. Bake for 30 to 40 minutes, basting occasionally with juice, until apples are tender but not mushy. Serve with whipped cream, if desired.

Glendeven Inn & Gallery
Little River, California

Sausage with Grapes

Six Servings

6 fresh sweet Italian sausages (about 1½ pounds)

2 cups seedless green grapes

Cut sausages into thirds. In a large covered skillet, cook sausages in 1 cup water for 10 minutes. Add grapes. Cover and simmer for 10 minutes. Uncover and cook over high heat until liquid begins to evaporate. Reduce heat and simmer uncovered for 15 to 20 minutes; drain. Serve with polenta, if desired.

Camellia Inn
Healdsburg, California

Zesty Salsa

Three Cups

3 ripe medium tomatoes, chopped

½ cup finely chopped onion

4 to 6 serrano chiles, finely chopped

½ cup fresh cilantro, finely chopped

2 teaspoons fresh lime juice

In a medium nonmetal bowl, combine tomatoes, onion, chiles, cilantro, and lime juice; stir well. Serve with eggs or breakfast potatoes.

Madrona Manor
Healdsburg, California

Breakfast Polenta

Twelve Servings

4 cups chicken broth

1 cup polenta (coarse cornmeal)

4 tablespoons butter

½ cup shredded cheddar or Swiss cheese

3 tablespoons butter, melted

¼ cup grated Parmesan cheese

In a large saucepan, bring chicken broth to a boil over high heat. Whisk in polenta. Reduce heat and simmer for for about 20 minutes, stirring frequently, until polenta becomes thick and pulls away from sides of pan. Add butter and cheese; stir until melted. Pour mixture into a greased 9- by 5-inch loaf pan. When cool, cover and refrigerate several hours or overnight.

Preheat oven to 350°F. Remove polenta from pan and cut into ¾-inch-thick slices. Cut slices in half diagonally and arrange in overlapping fashion in a greased shallow casserole dish. Drizzle with melted butter. Sprinkle with Parmesan cheese. Bake for 30 minutes, or until cheese is golden brown. Serve warm.

Gingerbread Mansion Inn
Ferndale, California

Baked Potato Latkes

Two Servings

1 medium baking potato

3 tablespoons vegetable oil

1 tablespoon grated onion

Salt to taste

⅛ teaspoon garlic powder

1 egg, separated

Applesauce and sour cream (optional)

Preheat oven to 450°F. Peel and grate potato into a bowl of cold water; let stand 30 minutes or longer. Grease a 12- by 9-inch baking pan with oil; preheat in oven for 10 minutes. Drain potatoes and squeeze out excess water. In a small bowl, combine potato with onion, salt, garlic powder, and egg yolk; mix well. In a separate bowl, beat egg white until very stiff. Drain excess liquid from potato mixture. Fold egg white into potato mixture. Spoon mixture into hot pan, forming 4 patties. Bake for 8 minutes, then flip patties and bake for 5 minutes, or until latkes are golden brown. Serve with warm applesauce and sour cream, if desired.

Wharfside Bed & Breakfast
Friday Harbor, Washington

German Potato Pancakes

Four Pancakes

2 medium boiling potatoes, peeled and grated

2 eggs, slightly beaten

2 tablespoons all-purpose flour

½ teaspoon salt

2 green onions, finely chopped

1 clove garlic, minced

1 tablespoon butter

Sour cream and applesauce (optional)

In a large bowl, combine potatoes, eggs, flour, salt, green onions, and garlic. In a 12-inch skillet, melt butter over medium heat. Divide batter into four patties and place in skillet. Cook patties for about 15 minutes over medium-low heat or until bottoms are golden brown. Turn and cook for 10 to 12 minutes, or until pancakes are golden brown. Serve with sour cream and applesauce, if desired.

Kristalberg Bed & Breakfast
Lucerne, California

Rosemary Roasted Potatoes

Four Servings

4 medium red potatoes, cut into ½-inch cubes

2 tablespoons olive oil

1 teaspoon dried sage

1 sprig fresh rosemary or 1 teaspoon crushed dried rosemary leaves

Zest of 1 orange

½ teaspoon pepper

Preheat oven to 375°F. Toss potatoes, oil, sage, rosemary, orange zest, and pepper in an ungreased 13- by 9-inch baking pan. Bake on center rack for 45 minutes, stirring occasionally, until potatoes are tender.

The Julian White House Bed & Breakfast
Julian, California

Home-Fried Potatoes and Peppers

Four Servings

3 cups diced baby red potatoes

2 tablespoons olive oil or clarified butter

1 cup diced red bell pepper

2 to 3 green onions, chopped

Dash seasoning salt

In a medium saucepan, cover potatoes with water and bring to boil. Reduce heat; cover and simmer for 4 to 5 minutes. Strain potatoes in a colander. In a large skillet, heat olive oil. Add potatoes and cook for 2 minutes without stirring. Add bell pepper and green onions; sauté until vegetables are tender and potatoes are evenly browned. Sprinkle with seasoning salt.

The Ballard Inn
Ballard, California

Index

A

Almonds
Cranberry Buttermilk Scones, 4
Easy Almond Pancakes, 60
Morning Muesli Mix, 84
Overnight French Toast, 77
Pear Almond Bread, 37
Angel Eggs, 113
Apple Cider Syrup, 153
Apples
Apfel Pfannkuchen, 61
Apple Cranberry Muffins, 22
Apple Oatmeal Crisp, 88
Apple Pecan French Toast, 74
Apple Pie Bread Pudding, 98
Apple Skillet Pancake, 95
Apple Walnut Pancakes, 57
Austrian Apple Strudel, 92
Baked Breakfast Apples, 166
Caramel Apple French Toast, 100
Cinnamon Apple Crepes, 64
Rise and Shine Oatmeal, 83
Applesauce Raisin Bread, 38
Applesauce Walnut Muffins, 15
Apricots
Apricot Cornmeal Muffins, 12
Austrian Apple Strudel, 92
Morning Muesli Mix, 84
Orange Apricot Muffins, 16
Artichoke Mushroom Bake, 130
Artichoke Mushroom Strata, 137
Austrian Apple Strudel, 92

B

Bacon
Bacon and Cheese Oven Omelet, 147
Easy Eggs Benedict, 117
Hash Brown Casserole, 144
Seashell Egg Bake, 115
Sunday Morning Casserole, 145
See also Ham
Baked Banana Crumble, 163
Baked Breakfast Apples, 166
Baked Cottage Cheese Pancake, 96
Baked Eggs. See Eggs, Baked
Baked Potato Latkes, 170

Bananas
Baked Banana Crumble, 163
Banana Buckwheat Pancakes, 56
Banana Pecan Bread, 39
Banana Walnut Bread Pudding, 99
Banana–Oat Bran Muffins, 18
Fresh Fruit Crepes, 65
Rise and Shine Oatmeal, 83
Belgian Waffles, Wild Rice, 69
Berries
Berry-Filled Scones, 8
Breakfast Berry Pudding, 97
Two Berry Sauce, 159
See also specific berry
Beverages
Delicious Date Shake, 152
Fresh Peach Smoothie, 151
Biscotti, Espresso, 104
Blackberries
Berry-Filled Scones, 8
Blackberry Syrup, 154
Broiled Sour Cream Blackberries, 164
Cran-Blackberry Muffins, 25
Blue Corn Pancakes with Pineapple Salsa, 62
Blueberries
Berry-Filled Scones, 8
Blueberry Cream Cheese Coffee Cake, 45
Blueberry Rhubarb Crisp, 87
Blueberry Sourdough Cobbler, 89
Blueberry Streusel Coffee Cake, 47
Breakfast Berry Pudding, 97
Broiled Sour Cream Blackberries, 164
Fluffy Blueberry Pancakes, 58
Fresh Blueberry Muffins, 11
Fresh Fruit Crepes, 65
Bread Pudding
Apple Pie Bread Pudding, 98
Banana Walnut Bread Pudding, 99
Breakfast Berry Pudding, 97
Breads & Coffee Cakes, 27–51
See also Bread Pudding; French Toast;
Pastries; Scones & Muffins
Breakfast Berry Pudding, 97
Breakfast Polenta, 169
Broiled Sour Cream Blackberries, 164
Brown Sugar Sunshine, 161
Buckwheat Buttermilk Waffles, 71
Buckwheat Pancakes, Banana, 56
Buns, Easy Sticky, 103
Butter, Hazelnut Honey, 156

C

Cake, Chocolate Zucchini Rum, 50
Caramel Apple French Toast, 100
Casseroles. *See* Eggs, Baked; Pies;
  Quiche & Frittatas
Caviar, Creamy Eggs with, 110
Cereals
  Crunchy Nut Granola, 86
  Morning Muesli Mix, 84
  Rise and Shine Oatmeal, 83
  Swiss Muesli, 85
Cheese
  Bacon and Cheese Oven Omelet, 147
  Baked Cottage Cheese Pancake, 96
  Baked Eggs with Two Cheeses, 122
  Cheese Blintz Soufflé, 102
  Cheesy Cornmeal Soufflé, 121
  Cheesy Spinach Delight, 140
  Chile Cheese Bake, 136
  Eggs Gruyère with Tomato Topping, 139
  Ham and Cheese Baked Eggs, 118
  Ham and Cheese Crustless Quiche, 127
  Mini Cheddar Cheese Soufflés, 119
  Miniature Ham and Cheese Quiches, 142
  Ricotta Pancakes, 59
  Smoked Salmon Cheesecake, 141
Cherries
  Blue Corn Pancakes with Pineapple Salsa, 62
  Crunchy Nut Granola, 86
  Dried Cherry Scones, 5
  Espresso Biscotti, 104
  Fresh Cherry Cobber, 90
  Morning Muesli Mix, 84
Chiles
  Angel Eggs, 113
  Baked Eggs for a Gang, 135
  Chile Cheese Bake, 136
  Chiles Rellenos Bake, 129
  Eye-Opener Jalepeño Corn Bread, 31
  Green Chile and Potato Pie, 126
  Ham and Cheese Crustless Quiche, 127
  South of the Border Crustless Quiche, 125
  Zesty Salsa, 168
Chocolate
  Chocolate Zucchini Bread, 42
  Chocolate Zucchini Rum Cake, 50
  Espresso Biscotti, 104
  Mimosa Truffles, 105
Cinnamon Apple Crepes, 64
Cinnamon Bread, Glazed, 29

Cinnamon Glazed Scones, 3
Cobblers. *See* Crisps & Cobblers
Coffee Cakes. *See* Breads & Coffee Cakes
Corn Bread, Eye-Opener Jalepeño, 31
Cornmeal
  Apricot Cornmeal Muffins, 12
  Blue Corn Pancakes with Pineapple Salsa, 62
  Breakfast Polenta, 169
  Cheesy Cornmeal Soufflé, 121
  Cornmeal and Oat Waffles, 67
  Eye-Opener Jalepeño Corn Bread, 31
Cottage Cheese Pancake, Baked, 96
Crab Soufflé, 120
Cranberries
  Apple Cranberry Muffins, 22
  Cranberry Buttermilk Scones, 4
  Cranberry Nut Bread, 40
  Cran-Blackberry Muffins, 25
  Espresso Biscotti, 104
  Morning Muesli Mix, 84
  Pumpkin Cranberry Coffee Cake, 49
Cream Cheese Coffee Cake, Blueberry, 45
Cream Cheese Coffee Cake, Raspberry, 43
Creamy Eggs with Caviar, 110
Crepes, Cinnamon Apple, 64
Crepes, Fresh Fruit, 65
Crisps & Cobblers
  Apple Oatmeal Crisp, 88
  Baked Banana Crumble, 163
  Blueberry Rhubarb Crisp, 87
  Blueberry Sourdough Cobbler, 89
  Fresh Cherry Cobber, 90
  Raspberry Kuchen, 91
Croissant French Toast, Decadent, 78
Croissants, Divine Filled, 112
Crumble, Baked Banana, 163
Crunchy Nut Granola, 86
Currants
  Baked Breakfast Apples, 166
  Blue Corn Pancakes with Pineapple Salsa, 62
  Oatmeal Buttermilk Pancakes, 55
  Orange Currant Scones, 9

D-E

Date Pecan Scones, 6
Date Shake, Delicious, 152
Dried Cherry Scones, 5
Easy Almond Pancakes, 60
Easy Eggs Benedict, 117
Easy Sticky Buns, 103

Eggs
  Angel Eggs, 113
  Creamy Eggs with Caviar, 110
  Divine Filled Croissants, 112
  Hawaiian Scramble, 111
  Poached Eggs Madison, 114
  Scrambled Eggs With Smoked Salmon, 109
  See also Eggs, Baked; Quiche & Frittatas;
    Soufflés
Eggs, Baked
  Artichoke Mushroom Bake, 130
  Artichoke Mushroom Strata, 137
  Bacon and Cheese Oven Omelet, 147
  Baked Eggs Florentine, 116
  Baked Eggs for a Gang, 135
  Baked Eggs with Two Cheeses, 122
  Cheesy Spinach Delight, 140
  Chile Cheese Bake, 136
  Chiles Rellenos Bake, 129
  Easy Eggs Benedict, 117
  Eggs Gruyère with Tomato Topping, 139
  Green Chile and Potato Pie, 126
  Ham and Cheese Baked Eggs, 118
  Hash Brown Casserole, 144
  Italian Zucchini Pie, 123
  Pepperoni Egg Casserole, 131
  Sausage Strata, 143
  Seashell Egg Bake, 115
  Smoked Salmon Cheesecake, 141
  Sunday Morning Casserole, 145
  See also Quiche & Frittatas; Soufflés
Espresso Biscotti, 104
Eye-Opener Jalapeño Corn Bread, 31

F
Fish & Shellfish
  Crab Soufflé, 120
  Creamy Eggs with Caviar, 110
  Divine Filled Croissants, 112
  Scrambled Eggs With Smoked Salmon, 109
  Smoked Salmon Cheesecake, 141
Fluffy Blueberry Pancakes, 58
French Breakfast Puffs, 10
French Toast
  Apple Pecan French Toast, 74
  Caramel Apple French Toast, 100
  Decadent Croissant French Toast, 78
  Lemon Poppy Seed French Toast, 72
  Orange Marnier French Toast, 75
  Overnight French Toast, 77

Peaches and Cream French Toast, 101
  Pineapple French Toast, 73
  Portuguese Peach French Toast, 79
  Surprise Stuffed French Toast, 76
Frittatas. *See* Quiche & Frittatas
Fruit Crepes, Fresh, 65

G–H
Gala Orange Sauce, 158
Garden Medley Quiche, 138
German Potato Pancakes, 171
Ginger Pear Muffins, 21
Ginger Sauce, Orange, 160
Gingerbread, Pumpkin, 34
Gingerbread Muffins, 19
Glazed Cinnamon Bread, 29
"Good Morning" Pie, 93
Granola. *See* Cereal
Grapefruit, in Brown Sugar Sunshine, 161
Grapes, Sausage With, 167
Green Chile and Potato Pie, 126
Ham
  Easy Eggs Benedict, 117
  Ham and Cheese Baked Eggs, 118
  Ham and Cheese Crustless Quiche, 127
  Hash Brown Quiche, 128
  Hawaiian Scramble, 111
  Miniature Ham and Cheese Quiches, 142
  Sunday Morning Casserole, 145
  See also Bacon
Hash Brown Casserole, 144
Hash Brown Quiche, 128
Hawaiian Breakfast Bread, 33
Hawaiian Scramble, 111
Hazelnuts
  Cran-Blackberry Muffins, 25
  Hazelnut Honey Butter, 156
  Hazelnut Waffles with Peaches, 66
Home-Fried Potatoes and Peppers, 173
Honey and Oats Bread, 30
Huckleberries
  Huckleberry Rhubarb Jam, 155
  Lemon Huckleberry Bread, 35
  Swedish Pancakes with Huckleberry Sauce, 63

I–L
Irish Soda Bread, 32
Italian Sausage Frittata, 146
Italian Zucchini Pie, 123
Jalapeño Corn Bread, Eye-Opener, 31

Jam, Huckleberry Rhubarb, 155
Kuchen, Raspberry, 91
Latkes, Baked Potato, 170
Lemons
    Lemon Curd, 157
    Lemon Huckleberry Bread, 35
    Lemon Poppy Seed French Toast, 72
    Mini Lemon Muffins, 20
    Raspberry Lemon Tea Bread, 41
Low-Fat Yogurt Muffins, 17

M–N

Mandarin Orange Muffins, 24
Marnier French Toast, Orange, 75
Mimosa Truffles, 105
Mini Cheddar Cheese Soufflés, 119
Mini Lemon Muffins, 20
Miniature Ham and Cheese Quiches, 142
Morning Muesli Mix, 84
Muesli, Swiss, 85
Muesli Mix, Morning, 84
Muffins. *See* Scones & Muffins
Mushrooms
    Artichoke Mushroom Bake, 130
    Artichoke Mushroom Strata, 137
    Divine Filled Croissants, 112
    Italian Sausage Frittata, 146
    Spinach Mushroom Quiche, 124
Nuts
    Cranberry Nut Bread, 40
    Crunchy Nut Granola, 86
    Strawberry Nut Bread, 36
    See also Almonds; Hazelnuts; Pecans; Walnuts

O

Oat Bran Muffins, Banana–, 18
Oatmeal
    Apple Oatmeal Crisp, 88
    Baked Banana Crumble, 163
    Blueberry Rhubarb Crisp, 87
    Cornmeal and Oat Waffles, 67
    Crunchy Nut Granola, 86
    Honey and Oats Bread, 30
    Morning Muesli Mix, 84
    Oatmeal Buttermilk Pancakes, 55
    Oatmeal Peach Muffins, 14
    Oatmeal Scones, 7
    Rise and Shine Oatmeal, 83
    Swiss Muesli, 85
Omelet, Bacon and Cheese Oven, 147

Oranges
    Dried Cherry Scones, 5
    Fresh Peach Smoothie, 151
    Gala Orange Sauce, 158
    "Good Morning" Pie, 93
    Mandarin Orange Muffins, 24
    Orange Apricot Muffins, 16
    Orange Currant Scones, 9
    Orange Ginger Sauce, 160
    Orange Marnier French Toast, 75
    Surprise Stuffed French Toast, 76
    Swiss Muesli, 85
Overnight French Toast, 77

P

Pancakes
    Apfel Pfannkuchen, 61
    Apple Skillet Pancake, 95
    Apple Walnut Pancakes, 57
    Baked Cottage Cheese Pancake, 96
    Banana Buckwheat Pancakes, 56
    Blue Corn Pancakes with Pineapple Salsa, 62
    Easy Almond Pancakes, 60
    Fluffy Blueberry Pancakes, 58
    German Potato Pancakes, 171
    Oatmeal Buttermilk Pancakes, 55
    Pear Dutch Baby, 94
    Ricotta Pancakes, 59
    Swedish Pancakes with Huckleberry Sauce, 63
    See also Waffles
Pastries
    Austrian Apple Strudel, 92
    Decadent Croissant French Toast, 78
    Divine Filled Croissants, 112
    Easy Sticky Buns, 103
    French Breakfast Puffs, 10
    Mimosa Truffles, 105
    See also Breads & Coffee Cakes
Peaches
    Fresh Fruit Crepes, 65
    Fresh Peach Smoothie, 151
    Hazelnut Waffles with Peaches, 66
    Oatmeal Peach Muffins, 14
    Overnight French Toast, 77
    Peaches and Cream French Toast, 101
    Portuguese Peach French Toast, 79
Pears
    Ginger Pear Muffins, 21
    Pear Almond Bread, 37
    Pear Dutch Baby, 94

Pears Extraordinaire, 162
Poached Pears in Raspberry Sauce, 165
Pecans
    Apple Pecan French Toast, 74
    Banana Pecan Bread, 39
    Caramel Apple French Toast, 100
    Crunchy Nut Granola, 86
    Date Pecan Scones, 6
    Easy Sticky Buns, 103
    Gingerbread Muffins, 19
    Mandarin Orange Muffins, 24
    Pumpkin Pie Muffins, 23
    Sour Cream Pecan Coffee Cake, 44
    Wild Rice Belgian Waffles, 69
Pepperoni. See Sausages
Pies
    Apple Pie Bread Pudding, 98
    "Good Morning" Pie, 93
    Green Chile and Potato Pie, 126
    Italian Zucchini Pie, 123
    Pear Dutch Baby, 94
    See also Eggs, Baked; Quiche & Frittatas
Pineapple
    Blue Corn Pancakes with Pineapple Salsa, 62
    Hawaiian Breakfast Bread, 33
    Hawaiian Scramble, 111
    Pineapple French Toast, 73
Plum Coffee Cake, Fresh, 46
Poached Eggs Madison, 114
Poached Pears in Raspberry Sauce, 165
Polenta, Breakfast, 169
Poppy Seed French Toast, Lemon, 72
Portuguese Peach French Toast, 79
Potatoes
    Baked Potato Latkes, 170
    German Potato Pancakes, 171
    Green Chile and Potato Pie, 126
    Hash Brown Casserole, 144
    Hash Brown Quiche, 128
    Home-Fried Potatoes and Peppers, 173
    Rosemary Roasted Potatoes, 172
Pudding, Bread. See Bread Pudding
Puffs, French Breakfast, 10
Pumpkins
    Pumpkin Cranberry Coffee Cake, 49
    Pumpkin Gingerbread, 34
    Pumpkin Pie Muffins, 23
    Pumpkin Spice Waffles, 68

Q-R
Quiche & Frittatas
    Garden Medley Quiche, 138
    Ham and Cheese Crustless Quiche, 127
    Hash Brown Quiche, 128
    Italian Sausage Frittata, 146
    Miniature Ham and Cheese Quiches, 142
    South of the Border Crustless Quiche, 125
    Spinach Mushroom Quiche, 124
    See also Eggs, Baked; Pies
Raisin Bread, Applesauce, 38
Raspberries
    Berry-Filled Scones, 8
    Breakfast Berry Pudding, 97
    Fresh Fruit Crepes, 65
    Overnight French Toast, 77
    Poached Pears in Raspberry Sauce, 165
    Raspberry Cream Cheese Coffee Cake, 43
    Raspberry Kuchen, 91
    Raspberry Lemon Tea Bread, 41
    Raspberry Streusel Muffins, 13
    Two Berry Sauce, 159
Rhubarb
    Blueberry Rhubarb Crisp, 87
    Huckleberry Rhubarb Jam, 155
    Rhubarb Buttermilk Coffee Cake, 48
Ricotta Pancakes, 59
Rise and Shine Oatmeal, 83
Rosemary Roasted Potatoes, 172
Rum Cake, Chocolate Zucchini, 50

S
Salmon. See Fish & Shellfish
Salsa, Pineapple, Blue Corn Pancakes with, 62
Salsa, Zesty, 168
Sauces & Side Dishes, 149–73
Sausages
    Italian Sausage Frittata, 146
    Pepperoni Egg Casserole, 131
    Sausage Strata, 143
    Sausage with Grapes, 167
Scones & Muffins, 1–25
Scrambled Eggs With Smoked Salmon, 109
Seashell Egg Bake, 115
Side Dishes. See Sauces & Side Dishes
Smoked Salmon Cheesecake, 141
Smoothie, Fresh Peach, 151

Soufflés
    Cheese Blintz Soufflé, 102
    Cheesy Cornmeal Soufflé, 121
    Crab Soufflé, 120
    Mini Cheddar Cheese Soufflés, 119
Sour Cream Blackberries, Broiled, 164
Sour Cream Pecan Coffee Cake, 44
South of the Border Crustless Quiche, 125
Spinach Delight, Cheesy, 140
Spinach Mushroom Quiche, 124
Sticky Bread Coffee Cake, 51
Sticky Buns, Easy, 103
Strawberries
    Broiled Sour Cream Blackberries, 164
    Decadent Croissant French Toast, 78
    Strawberry Nut Bread, 36
    Two Berry Sauce, 159
    Whole Wheat Waffles, 70
Strudel, Austrian Apple, 92
Sunday Morning Casserole, 145
Surprise Stuffed French Toast, 76
Swedish Pancakes with Huckleberry Sauce, 63
Swiss Muesli, 85
Syrup, Apple Cider, 153
Syrup, Blackberry, 154

T–Z

Truffles, Mimosa, 105
Two Berry Sauce, 159
Waffles
    Buckwheat Buttermilk Waffles, 71
    Cornmeal and Oat Waffles, 67

    Hazelnut Waffles with Peaches, 66
    Pumpkin Spice Waffles, 68
    Whole Wheat Waffles, 70
    Wild Rice Belgian Waffles, 69
    See also Pancakes
Walnuts
    Apple Walnut Pancakes, 57
    Applesauce Raisin Bread, 38
    Applesauce Walnut Muffins, 15
    Austrian Apple Strudel, 92
    Banana Walnut Bread Pudding, 99
    Banana–Oat Bran Muffins, 18
    Blueberry Cream Cheese Coffee Cake, 45
    Chocolate Zucchini Rum Cake, 50
    Espresso Biscotti, 104
    Fresh Plum Coffee Cake, 46
    Ginger Pear Muffins, 21
    Oatmeal Peach Muffins, 14
    Pumpkin Pie Muffins, 23
    Rhubarb Buttermilk Coffee Cake, 48
    Strawberry Nut Bread, 36
Whole Wheat Waffles, 70
Wild Rice Belgian Waffles, 69
Zesty Salsa, 168
Zucchini
    Chocolate Zucchini Bread, 42
    Chocolate Zucchini Rum Cake, 50
    Italian Zucchini Pie, 123

About The Author

Carol Frieberg has pursued her passion for healthful living in the food, health, and wellness field for 25 years. She is a former food editor for General Mills, Inc., and a spokesperson for Betty Crocker. Carol has authored four cookbooks and has made numerous media appearances, including book signings, cooking demonstrations, radio talk shows, and national television broadcasts.

Frieberg is currently a culinary consultant, with ongoing engagements in the production of local and national food and lifestyle television segments. She lives in Seattle, where she enjoys sharing her enthusiasm for food that is fresh, healthy, and simply prepared.